Captain Madness

Captain Madness

Living the Life of Riley

A thought-provoking and hilarious memoir journey
that will challenge your ultimate life choices.

DARE TO BE YOURSELF

EDWIN RILEY Ph.D.

Also by Edwin Riley, Ph.D.

EARTHWISE: An Approach To Planetary Sanity & Eco-Journal

The Alphabet Soup For Stress Reduction

Stress Rx: 103 Prescriptions For Overcoming Stress
and Achieving Lifelong Happiness

Fat Rx

Confront Reality: You May Be A Salad

Go Naked To The Market

Cover design, editing and interior formatting by Elyse Rich
Photographs by Captain Madness et al.
Published by Creative Adventures Publishing
Printed in the United States of America

PRAISES FOR
Captain Madness

Captain Madness is no ordinary memoir—told in the ancient spirit of the Irish poet tradition, it captures you like a judge in a 'Court of Consciousness' and pulls you into a life fully lived.

Edwin's instinct-fueled odyssey awakens your own courage to choose passion over stagnation and movement over mere existence. Read it, share it, and be reborn into the adventure only you can live.

—*Viktoras Kulvinskas,* PhD, DD, MS
Co-Founder, Hippocrates Health Institute
Author of *Survival in the 21st Century*

"Having known Edwin Riley for many years, I've always admired his boundless curiosity and irreverent spirit—both of which shine brilliantly in *Captain Madness: Living the Life of Riley.*

This fiercely honest and often laugh-out-loud memoir—his hilarious encounter with Hunter S. Thompson hits close to home—charts a life of intuition over convention, revealing wisdom in the wild, grace in the absurd, and what it truly means to live freely and authentically."

—*Mitchell Kaplan*
Founder, Owner, Books & Books
Co-Founder, *Miami Book Fair*

Dedication

To Anne Sue,
for believing in me.
and HA! HA! to those who didn't.

TABLE OF CONTENTS

FOREWORD

Captain Madness: Living the Life of Riley is a blueprint for living—reminding us that life's meaning is not found in destinations, but in how we walk the path itself.

It speaks to the eternal truth that to know oneself is to step into the mystery, to risk, to trust, and to live with presence in the great unfolding of existence.

Every true teaching carries its own syncopation—it finds us when we are ready, and never a moment too soon.

Captain Madness holds a timeless wisdom that only comes from lived experience, the kind that deepens when we surrender to the present moment, release our attachments, and allow serendipity to be our guide.

The only prerequisite for a life of adventure is complete trust in the Way—that quiet knowing that there is a divine order, and that everything, even the unexpected, has its place in perfection.

Captain Madness is a call to adventure: to live life fully, to break free from conformity, and to dive boldly into spiritual exploration. There is an artful rhythm between being a free spirit and taking conscious, deliberate risks.

Edwin Riley embodies this with brilliance—never too entangled, always attuned, and forever keeping his finger on the pulse of life.

Edwin's voice carries a cadence all its own—easy, unhurried, and rich with the melodic quirks of Southern storytelling.

There's a playful drawl in his prose, a winking rhythm that softens even the sharpest truths. His words meander like a backroad conversation, winding through wisdom, humor, and the occasional poetic detour—always landing exactly where they're meant to, in their own sweet time.

What makes his words especially powerful is that he lived them: embracing uncertainty with courage, finding joy in the unplanned, and turning every twist in the road into an opening for discovery.

Though written 25 years ago, these words could just as easily have been written today and will be just as relevant in years to come. That is the nature of true insight—it transcends time, carrying within it the breath of the eternal.

This work captures the essence of the human journey: the search for self, the discovery of eternal messages, and the joy of riding the unpredictable waves of existence. Like surfers carried by tides of energy and vibe, we are reminded that life is an ocean inviting us to glide, explore, and awaken.

As you enter these pages, may you feel inspired to listen more deeply, live more freely, and discover your own adventure waiting within.

Ever onward,
Elyse Rich
Futurist, Artist, Visionary

Living the Life of Riley.

INTRODUCTION
Writing On The Wind

"These are my Buddha songs.
This time I will sing them to paper."
— from the Captain's Log

H ere I am, facing the existential white void. Writing a book. Perhaps the most daunting endeavor imaginable known to any relatively sane human being.

All my writing tools are gathered around—yellow legal pads, pens, computer, Webster's gigantic unabridged dictionary, a thesaurus, tape recorder. I even purchased sophisticated, state-of-the-art software that transcribes recorded text.

Distractions have been removed except for my companion, who generates erotic thoughts seducing my mind away from the desolate blank page.

Yet she is an integral part of the process, providing both technical and moral support.

Like rum drinks in the afternoon, I will not give up certain pleasures, including the fantasies.

There must be balance, yin and yang, such as making love when the mood strikes OR writing a book.

These lustful days of newfound romance are part of my own creative expression.

Perhaps I'll next write about these spirited ventures into the physical realm.

Make this my focus. My meditation.

Sex as mantra.

Besides, she is the one who talked me into this madness.

I had long been perfectly content to write on the wind, letting words flow from soulful creation to cosmic vibrations.

Buddha sang songs sitting beneath the Bodhi tree.

There is no testimonial sheet music as personal historical record. He composed to the cosmos.

I believe, much to the ire of my writer friends, that this is the purest, most exquisite form of egoless creative expression.

If we write in our minds and let it go, the creative energy generates vibrations affecting the entire planet, not just a handful of readers.

She, like many other friends and strangers, has long pleaded with me to write stories I have lived.

My life's journey is a tapestry of adrenaline soul-seeking adventures and miscues. It has been a quest for the meaningfulness of life and evolution of mind, body, and spirit.

I remember the day that I made the conscious decision to follow such a path, knowing it would not be easy, that I would live and die thousands of times in the risk-taking process.

Such is the heavy tariff.

But a much greater debt would be looking back in my later years with regret for not having lived fully.

Along the way I have been a journalist, professor, yacht captain, furniture mover. I've also been a circus clown, radio disc jockey, bartender, father, psychotherapist, poet, actor, and many other worldly incarnations.

In the process, I have pissed off a lot of people who resent my free spirit. I have long given up trying to please everyone.

I take personal responsibility for my own well-being and divinity.

Now, more than ever, I focus on living fully in the present moment utilizing all my senses, insights, and intuition.

There are so many wonderful lessons to learn in this dance of life if we open ourselves to being fully present.

I admiringly embrace the philosophy of Henry David Thoreau and the spirit of Jack Kerouac.

While seemingly contradictory personalities, both Thoreau and Kerouac chose to live life deliberately.

For this reason, I am calling this book: *The Life of Riley— On the Road with Thoreau, On Track with Kerouac.*

My mission, as I interpret it, is as a "raconteur."

For all intents and purposes, I am a storyteller.

First and foremost.

My intention is to share the magic and serendipity that results when we march to the beat of our own drummer.

These are MY Buddha songs.

This time I will sing them to paper.

I hope you enjoy the melody.

Title Change in 2025 to Captain Madness

UPDATED AUTHOR'S INTRODUCTION (2025)

To set the record straight, time is constantly changing—as are we. Because I wrote most of *Captain Madness* 25 years ago, many social mores ring a different bell. Definitions of liberal and conservative today in 2025 are reversed or, at best, maligned.

Captain Madness is a memoir—a telling reflection on many life adventures and soul searching that I pass on as my legacy to you, the reader.

Stories refer to **THAT** timeframe; gems sometimes caught in a time warp. Many of the characters in my stories are no longer inhabiting planet Earth.

I trust you will experience interwoven insights about life itself, what it has to offer, and the importance of living optimally with love and compassion as your baseline. And if you can't sit in truth without unreasonable squirming, pass your copy onto someone who can laugh and skip life's ropes.

I am a raconteur. Aside from entertainment value, *Captain Madness* is about harnessing storytelling to empower personal growth and transformation. I couldn't find a book I wanted to read—just old, worn-out mystery novels with predictable endings—so I wrote my own, for my own enjoyment and pleasure—and hopefully yours, too.

Peace, Love, and Laughter

Captain Madness

What? Me worry?

DISCLAIMER

All the people I write about are real.
So are their names and these stories.
They were partners in life.

—I hope my lawyer is as good as he claims.

Scoring a South Carolina backroads delicacy.

SERENDIPITY

"Funny how things unfold if you just let them."
— from the Captain's Log

S hit happens. So does magic. Like most of us, I prefer magic. For "magic" to prevail, we must be in flow. What this means is living like a leaf effortlessly winding its way downstream on a meandering river of unexpected twists and turns.

The leaf does not struggle; it moves with ease around boulders and logs, in currents and eddies, on its pathway to whatever comes next.

Perhaps, with this stream, the leaf finds its way to the next tributary. Ultimately, water carries leaf to sea, an infinite expanse of freedom on this planet.

We are like a leaf on the rivers and seas of life.

If we are in flow, our journey seems effortless, and we are rewarded in our surrender to unexplained circumstances as seemingly unrelated events come together in time.

This is called "synchronicity" and "serendipity."

If we try to control our fate, believing we're steering the river, we end up struggling against nature and freedom, clinging to obstacles along the way.

In 1973, while in graduate school at the University of Florida, a series of events occurred that some people might initially consider "coincidental" at best.

I call it magic, and my surrender to these encounters and experiences became a turning point in my life.

Funny how things unfold if you just let them. I had decided in the fall of 1972 that I "had to" spend some time next summer at the *Jack Kerouac School of Disembodied Poetics.*

A six-week program held at the Naropa Institute in Boulder, Colorado, this highfalutin' name, designated by Allen Ginsberg, undeniably the greatest American poet since Walt Whitman, had become an experiential font of foment and introspection.

The common denominator attracting beat writers was Chögyam Trungpa Rinpoche, reputedly the 17th incarnate in a lineage of enlightened Buddhist leaders.

His schtick, however, was based on what he called "crazy wisdom." That's how he justified drinking massive amounts of sake and driving his Porsche through the plate-glass window of a toy store, leaving him with a limp in his left leg until his untimely death of heart failure on April 4th, 1987, in Nova Scotia at age 47.

My wife was less than enthusiastic about my decision.

Beat writers have always been known for their freewheeling, spontaneous lifestyles. This historically includes sex, drugs, and a lack of inhibition. The Beat creed focuses on finding oneself, which more often than not means dropping time-honored societal mores and institutionalized thinking.

Being a father of two children, I found that the word "responsibility" kept entering conversations. I took the word then to mean doing something unpleasant and forced upon us.

Somehow this didn't suit.

Some 21 years later, while interning at the Center for Mindfulness at the University of Massachusetts Medical

School, I learned that responsibility literally means "to respond to."

It has nothing whatsoever to do with being someone you are not, trying to fit into a box created by institutions hell-bent on keeping the masses in check.

Going against the grain takes a lot of courage, fortitude, and internal strength. Also, a stubborn streak and hard-headed self-will. But more than that, beyond the superficial, it rises from the depth of one's individual soul, with a sense of longing probably thousands of years in process.

I KNEW I had to go there, to Boulder, Colorado, for the six-week program, even though I could not in convincing terms verbalize this internal passion and desire.

More than just a whim, I KNEW it was an integral journey in my evolution of time spent on this planet.

The next major step.

No one in my family seemed to appreciate, much less understand, such logic.

Support came from several esoteric university friends. One influential person in particular was English professor David Rebmann, who several years later was denied tenure for "relating too closely to his students."

Mostly, it had to do with him living with his student after his wife and children moved out. Plus, he wore his prematurely gray hair in a long ponytail and often held classes in his now-empty living room, always opening the session with sitting meditation, usually led by me. He DID relate to his students, and they loved him for it.

Long-term academics make for strange bedfellows. As time passes, they lose the verve that may have brought them into the fold initially. They teach by rote, become complacent, and turn into pedantic boors.

Unlike one might think and hope, most colleges and universities do not encourage free thought, especially today. Insecure, egomaniacal, small-minded pissants generally rule them. This may be too kind a declaration, and I have a volume of anecdotes to back me up.

Enough venting... for now, anyway. David and I quickly became close friends, especially after he and I took a road trip during Christmas break to visit my brother, who was living on his sailboat at Boot Key Marina in the Florida Keys.

On the road, I introduced David to boiled peanuts. Being originally from Connecticut, he kept disdainfully calling them "goobers" until we got south of Miami, after making quite an indention in the lid of "Gainesville Green," a cruise-control kind of marijuana locally grown in Gainesville, Florida.

By the time we reached Key Largo, boiled peanuts were David's favorite cuisine, and he couldn't get enough. He enjoys them immensely to this day.

While on this venture, we decided to design and co-teach a new course at the University. I had recently been kicked out of the creative writing program for challenging an establishment professor and visiting lecturer, who just happened to be the long-time poetry editor for the *Saturday Review.*

My seminar peers sided with my point of view as to the validity of metaphysical and stream-of-consciousness poetry with such enthusiasm that I was labeled a malcontent.

It took a full year and a summer to remove me from the elitist-minded program, and the chicken-shit administrators exiled me to the College of Education, where l was required to intern, teaching two courses for graduation.

David had attended the *Jack Kerouac School of Disembodied Poetics* at Naropa the summer before. In fact, he roomed with William Burroughs, Jr., and, on many occasions, tied his hands and feet to the bedposts so Burroughs could cold-turkey the demons of excessive alcohol and drugs of choice.

It was during one of our boiled peanut and Gainesville Green-fueled inspirational moments that we arrived at the course title *Literature of the Beat Generation* and divvied up who would teach which writers.

One afternoon, I was sitting in Professor David's office, pontificating about how we would continue co-teaching our course, *Literature of the Beat Generation.* He asked how we might "spice up" the class. I suggested we call San Francisco poet Lawrence Ferlinghetti and ask if he would join us for a conference telephone interview.

When asked how we should go about making this happen, I reached for the phone and asked the operator to connect us with City Lights Bookstore, Ferlinghetti's business and a legendary gathering spot for the Beat writers. When I was connected, I asked to speak to Lawrence Ferlinghetti.

"This is Larry Ferlinghetti," he said.

"Well, I'm Edwin Riley at the University of Florida, and I'm preparing to discuss your book, *A Coney Island of the Mind,* with my class. Will you consider a conference call with the students?"

This set the wheels of magic—synchronicity—in motion.

As a former journalist and public relations man, I reflected on how to get mileage out of the conference call.

I contacted the Independent Florida Alligator, a popular daily off-campus newspaper, and spoke with the editor, who assigned a reporter to cover the class.

"Mister Ferlinghetti, what are you working on now?" the first student asked.

"Right now," he replied, "I'm working on rolling a joint."

Marijuana was newly hip on college campuses in the early seventies, and students found his answer bonding.

"What I really want to know," Ferlinghetti continued, "is why you're talking to me when Howard Odum is in your own backyard. That's who the Beats are listening to."

Who the hell is Howard Odum? We were all perplexed.

So was Howard Odum when the newspaper article appeared the next day. His right-hand man called: What does research professor Dr. Odum have in common with Beat writers like Ferlinghetti, Allen Ginsberg, Jack Kerouac, and this menagerie of social anarchists?

"Why don't you come to my class, and let's figure it out," I suggested.

Later that day, we sat at an outside table at the Library, a local bar on University Avenue, excitedly downing pitchers of draft beer and plotting an event we dubbed—
Energy Consciousness Weekend: A Celebration of Ecological Consciousness at the Spring Equinox.

We had figured out the common ground between Beats and Odum. Odum, a well-respected research professor, promoted steady-state economics. The message was economically Thoreau-like.

- Simplify, simplify.
- Stop destroying the planet.
- No more depletion of fossil fuels.
- Seek alternative solutions.
- Take responsibility for planetary concerns.

Our meeting with Odom's representative was indeed fortuitous. We decided to bring these formidable forces of both the arts and sciences together.

The wheels were in motion.

Ferlinghetti couldn't come.

He had a prior engagement in Prague.

We invited Allen Ginsberg; Pulitzer-prize winner Gary Snyder; and poet/playwright Michael McClure to attend.

We, meaning David and I, solicited Student Government for support since the University wasn't enthusiastic to fund an event that might actually lure proven talent with hostile points of view to establishment dogma.

The Beats were so anxious to hold the symposium with Odum they agreed to come for the paltry sum of $200 and airfare. Local songster Dale Crider put them up at his home in the country.

In addition to the symposium held in the University auditorium, one night would include a poetry reading outside at Graham Pond, a pristine sinkhole that's in front of the women's dorm.

It was a particularly environmentally seductive location, where students and attendees could sit on this hillside surrounding the still water.

Much to the dismay of the creative writing department's cretins, I was chosen as one of four Florida poets to read that evening.

En route to the symposium, I was riding with Ginsberg and his friend from Santa Fe, David Padwa, who had flown in on the plane with him.

Padwa had seen a campus poster announcing next week's arrival of Ram Dass, aka the legendary Dr. Richard Alpert, Harvard drop-out and pop guru.

Alpert was best known for his early scientifically controlled LSD experiments with the iconic Timothy Leary, and for his seminal book *Be Here Now*.

The classic sixties book details messages of importance for living in the present moment as insightfully gained via a pilgrimage to India. There, Ram Dass and the young Laguna Beach surfing soul seeker—who would soon change his name to Bhagavan Das—met Neem Karoli Baba, Ram Dass's mentor.

Padwa was new to this particular scene, having met Ram Dass while teaching Chinese economics at Harvard. They had become close friends with a mutual interest in Eastern philosophy and religion.

Padwa embraced Buddhism and invited Tibetan lamas to his home in the Santa Fe foothills. The lamas even brought a chorten, a meditation monument from Tibet, and erected it on Padwa's lot adjacent to his home.

"If you see Richard next week," Padwa said turning to me, "tell him I said hello. It has been some time since we have seen one another."

In response to my curiosity about their acquaintance, he asked if I had read *Be Here Now*.

In the book, the young Laguna Beach surfer had run off with a Land Rover and presented it as an offering to the Indian guru, Neem Karoli Baba.

The Land Rover, it seems, belonged to Padwa, who at the time was unaware of this "gifting."

I had read the book many times over.

"Tell me," I asked, "is it true what is written in the book, that Neem Karoli Baba existed on a diet of six almonds and goat milk?"

Padwa looked me in the eyes.

"Naw," he said. "That's just a teaching metaphor that Richard uses."

"Hummmmm," I responded. "Always been curious as to whether that was literal."

When Ram Dass arrived, I heard him speak. I learned he was giving an informal talk on the community college campus the next day, so I joined the small group of students sitting on the lawn under a huge oak awaiting his arrival. A cool spring breeze was blowing in the midday air. Not one for cold, I decided to move about 15 feet away into the sunshine.

There I was, sitting cross-legged in my orange butterfly shirt and sandalwood beads, when Ram Dass came strolling up the hill, trailed by his student entourage.

He paused under the tree where the students had gathered, then turned and looked directly at me sitting in my half lotus, face raised to the sun. Without an utterance, he came over to where I was sitting and plopped down face to face, everyone scurrying now to join us in the sun.

"Sun feels great," I said.

He nodded in accord.

After his talk, we stood and began walking down the hill toward campus.

"I met a friend of yours last week. David Padwa. He said to tell you hello," I said.

"Ah, David, haven't seen him in a year. How was he and what was he doing here?"

I told him the story, stopped for a moment to reflect on what I really wanted to ask, then recounted my conversation with David about Neem Karoli Baba subsisting off six almonds and goat's milk.

"He said it was your teaching metaphor," I said.

Ram Dass stopped in his tracks.

"David said that?" he asked with some incredulity.

I nodded my head, and we resumed our walk.

Ram Dass stopped again.

"David is a very linear person," he said, looking me straight in the eyes. "He is a businessman and a very good one. That experience was out of his reality. So, what he probably saw was Baba eating a steak, baked potato and salad... Do you understand what I am saying?"

"Yes," I replied. I had come to realize many people are limited in thinking and only see and hear what their belief systems allow. Reality is short-changed.

Much of this is fear based.

We started walking again.

Ram Dass continued, "But the truth is, Baba only ate six almonds and drank goat's milk when we were present."

I realized after my conversations with both of these brilliant individuals that I had opened tremendously to how we, as individuals, perceive not only others and ourselves, but also the world in which we live.

I was beginning to admit how we can delude ourselves in illusions and distortions and habitual thought patterns created for mass consumption.

David and Ram Dass were perfect examples. Each one saw something differently. Perhaps neither one, I thought, saw through their eyes and minds the actuality.

What had begun as a thought seedling back in November had evolved to a course of action. I had known that I somehow, for some unexplainable reason, needed to be there.

Then my conversation happened with Ferlinghetti, which led to the newspaper article, followed by *Energy Consciousness Weekend*, and insistence from those attending to be at Naropa for the six-week Kerouac convening.

My encounter with David Padwa, his connection to Ginsberg and Eastern thinking, plus his invitation to be his guest in Santa Fe, New Mexico, marked another turning point even though that destination was far from my mind at the time.

L-R: David Padwa, Michael McClure, and me.
Professor David Rebmann in the background.

Allen Ginsberg: Poet. Activist.

Allen Ginsberg, Gary Snyder,
Michael McClure, and Howard Odum.

Opening a new chapter in my life.

CUTTING THE TIE THAT BINDS

*"You either do it, or you die. Maybe not immediate physical death,
but one more chronic, numbing, and forever on this earth plane."*
— from the Captain's Log

Before returning to graduate studies at the University of Florida, we had purchased a VW van. Having two cars, I now focused on preparing the van for my trip west. I could use it as shelter when necessary.

My wife preferred driving our other car anyway.

This would be my "on the road" experience, living briefly as a dharma bum, traveling cross-country with my guitar, bicycle, stereo, stove, typewriter, and cooler.

I was searching for meaningfulness to those larger questions of life we all, as human beings confined to this small planet, periodically ask.

Mind you, my proposed trip had not gained any support from family. Quite the contrary. The word "responsibility" was my scarlet letter, emblazoned repeatedly and vengefully on my soul and psyche.

Mind-tripping and manipulation upped the ante. Much as I desired for them to understand, because to me, in all my heart, I felt it was a decision much greater than myself I was unable to articulate this divine intervention.

My words somehow lacking and defensive in my quest as I moved forward.

My van project was completed. I had built a padded bed. Its underneath housed storage for food and my guitar. I was ready for travel, now less than a month away.

"If you think you're taking the van," the wife said, "then forget it."

Hers was a last-minute stand, like the Alamo. We had both dug our feet deep into our feelings. We sat on the couch.

In what seemed an eternity, I tried to explain what mere words couldn't breach.

"Just regard this as a marital separation," I finally said.

We held each other and cried.

Many things in life are painful, yet necessary. Perhaps the worst is leaving behind those you love to do something you can't fully explain, not to them and not even to yourself.

You either do it, or you die.

Maybe not immediate physical death, but one more chronic, numbing, and forever on this earth plane, usually accompanied with inappropriate action.

This is Death of Spirit. We see it everywhere: the vacant eyes, depression, aggression, greed, obsessive behavior, gross materialism, power struggles, manipulation, low self-esteem, lack of self-worth.

There is a long list for the absence of love and search for truth.

The next afternoon, my phone rang. I preferred riding my bicycle to campus rather than taking the car and had just walked through the front door, drenched in sweat.

It was my friend Edith. I had told her my van story earlier at class. She was concerned that I was undisturbed, even elated, as I said with sincerity that it really didn't matter. This was just a test. I would hitchhike to Boulder.

"Have you read today's Florida Alligator?" she asked excitedly. (The off-campus daily newspaper was more popular and widely read than the city's daily.)

"Just walked in," I said.

There was an ad from a celebrated nuclear research professor, Dr. Stanislaw Ulam, looking for a "responsible" person to deliver his new car to Boulder, Colorado.

There was that word again... "responsible."

Ironic, I thought. I've had it thrown at me, and now it is presenting itself before me. I called, got directions, and drove immediately to his home.

Ulam, as it turned out, had worked with Edward Teller in Los Alamos, New Mexico, on the development of the atomic bomb. He and his French writer wife, Francoise, spent the winter semester in Gainesville, then alternated between Santa Fe, New Mexico, and Boulder, Colorado.

They would pay gas fare if I drove their car. I even had the option: Santa Fe or Boulder.

Serendipity. I had let go of trying to force something to happen yet had not given up.

David Padwa had invited me to Santa Fe. My destination was Boulder. I was graduating two weeks before the program at Naropa began. Now the window was wide open.

Earlier today, I was willing to walk across country. Why not do both? Drive to Santa Fe, then thumb the last 400 miles across Independent Pass to Boulder.

My bike would be sold to buy a sleeping bag and backpack. I intended to travel light. My other baggage was my guitar. In its case, I crammed two books: Patanjali's *Yoga Sutras* and Pirsig's *Zen and the Art of Motorcycle Maintenance*.

I also carried a cotton Peruvian shoulder bag with my journal. On the inside cover were inscribed two quotes, one by Henry David Thoreau and the other by French essayist Montaigne. I would refer to them frequently on my journey for reassurance and as a reminder of my quest.

The parting goodbye was expectedly tearful. I had already been forewarned that "my stuff" might not be there when I returned. Neither would they. This was harsh reality.

I was leaving my life up to now, with all its certainties and predictable comforts and pitfalls, in my wake. I knew that once I drove away, I might never again have the option to resume what I was leaving. Life would never be the same.

Yet then again, it already was not the same.

What had been in past years had changed, as all things do. Change is inevitable. We all say this but seldom pause to analyze the ingredients. Often, we are baffled at outcomes not "in our plans."

How did this or that possibly happen?

If we don't pay attention, we may never see it coming. Lack of being aware is an affliction as deadly as any chronic illness. And being attached to outcomes, as if somehow, we are in control every moment of our lives, is perhaps the greatest fallacy.

Living in the past can be deadly. We miss living entirely.

Every breath we take is new and different. Several minutes without presence of breath brings about another, entirely different, kind of change we label "death."

This, too, is harsh reality. We usually look in other directions, either past or future, afraid of being fully present in the moment riding each breath, even though past is history and future is not available.

In trying to understand more about the meaning of life, I gaze out to sea, watching wave after wave, each one different, no two the same, moving effortlessly to the shore.

No two of us alike, each person unique with our own fingerprints, voice, footprints; our own DNA. Never before in all history has there been anyone exactly like any one of us. I find this very consoling. Perhaps this was the constitutional message in "All men are created equal."

Our bodies are more than 75 per cent water, a saline solution like the sea. We have the ocean within us. Like waves on the ocean, driven by forces of nature, wind and tides, moon phases and storms, we have little actual control on our lives other than being fully aware in any given moment of our presence, intentions, and actions.

We have choice, free will, to surf the oceans of ourselves or struggle against the inevitable forces of nature within ourselves.

As my wife and I pulled our bodies apart, looked into each other's tear-filled eyes, and I turned to walk down the stairway, her parting, words etched like beach sand in this rite of passage, rang after me: "I hope you find what you're looking for."

I looked back and said, "So do I."

The ride across country to Santa Fe was tumultuous. Like riding an emotional bucking bronco, I kept clinging to the past. Memories surfaced, and the more I dwelled on "what ifs" and "nevermore," the more I created my own turbulent sea.

My decision to become an explorer and discover what living life to its fullest had to reveal produced an enormous amount of societal guilt.

Intuitively, I knew I was doing the right thing.

Conditionally, I was terrified. Even today in my knowing, I still bear emotional scars. This is part of being human in a perfect world that we perceive as imperfect. I can accept this weighty contradiction.

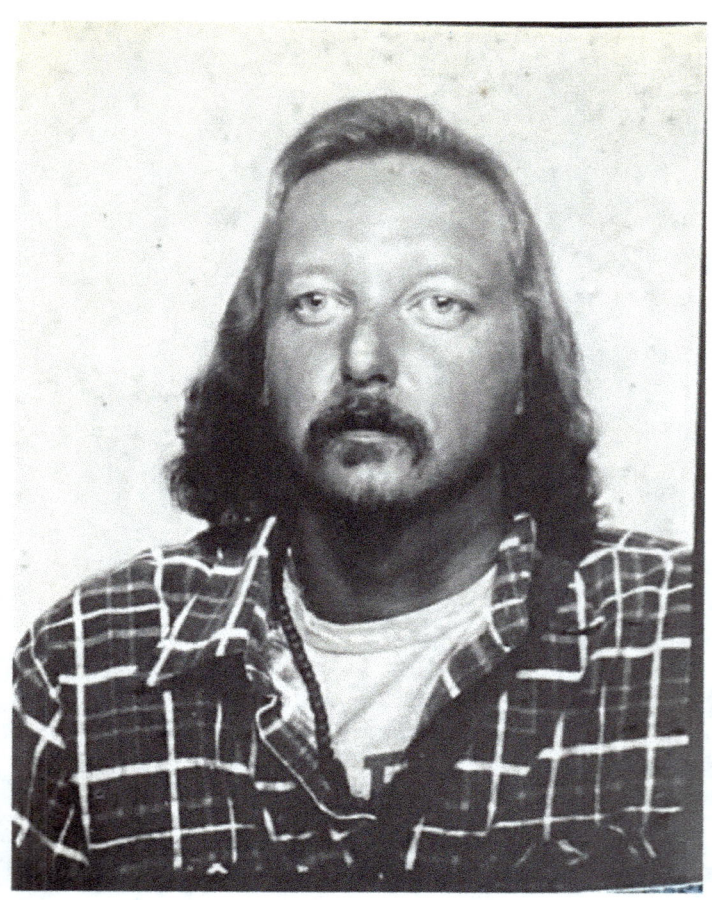

"What do you mean you never learned to drive?!"

RIDE BOARD CONNIE

"Sometimes the ride is the lesson."
— from the Captain's Log

Some people like to drive. They feel more in control. I don't. My preference is going along for the ride. This is my metaphor for life in general.

A cross-country solo drive seemed formidable.

I decided to stop in Tallahassee and check out the ride board in the student union at Florida State University. Students are always going somewhere. Maybe I would find someone heading west.

Sure enough. Connie had posted a notice "Seeking ride to Boulder, Colorado." Serendipity. Here I was, heading to Boulder, with an option to drop off the car in Santa Fe, which I had pretty much decided to do, and I had a potential passenger. There was no phone, only an address and directions.

I was elated.

A coed to share the driving and conversation across country. Too good to be true. What a beginning, an omen.

That was until I picked up Ride Board Connie, who was sleeping on the floor of an old frame house near the campus.

We were heading along the Gulf Coast towards Alabama. "I'll drive first," I volunteered, "then you can take over." She didn't even have to put up gas money, just drive more than her share. She would certainly be ecstatic.

"I don't know how to drive," she informed me.

"I never learned."

31

This was incredible! Every teenager wants to drive. I got my South Carolina's driver's license at fourteen. Had to look between the horn and steering wheel to see the road.

"Well, guess what," I told her. "You're going to learn." I'm usually the good guy in situations involving the opposite sex. Sir Galahad. But this time was going to be different, despite her pleas of helplessness.

Just as I was starting to question my "serendipity," we passed a highway patrol station. Quickly I turned around and pulled in. "We're getting you a learner's permit," I explained.

For reasons I can't fully remember, she didn't get the permit but consented to driving lessons once we hit an open stretch of highway. Texas was especially easy. Nothing but open road. By then she had learned how not to drive on the shoulder and stay in her lane.

Ride Board Connie was a pain in the ass.

She preferred crocheting to conversation. When she did talk, she complained. And in the end, she was argumentative about my decision to drop the car in New Mexico up to the very last minute when I let her off at the bus station.

Small waves at Canaveral Pier East Coast Surfing competition.

THE LAGUNA BEACH SURFER

"Some meetings change your path. Others change your pace."
— from the Captain's Log

David Padwa's number was in the phone book. He answered the ring seemingly non-plussed at my unannounced arrival in Santa Fe and invited me to his home. "Go past the drive and park next to the fence", he instructed. "You will see the meditation monument. Walk clockwise around it 108 times, and then come on down to the house," he further instructed.

As I got out of the car, a pick-up truck came roaring out of the driveway and backed up the dusty hill to where I was standing at the chorten's entrance.

"Hi," the young woman said. "I'm David's wife. David had to go into town to meet Lama Tinley," she explained. "After you meditate, walk on down to the house. Bhagavan Das is there."

Serendipity strikes again. Bhagavan Das was the Laguna Beach surfer dude Padwa had told me about who had stolen David's Land Rover as a gift to Neem Karoli Baba. The kid in the book, *Be Here Now*.

Bhagavan Das was tall and slender except for a protruding belly. He wore shoulder-length, blonde scraggly hair and seashell earrings in both ears. He had spent the summer before at the *Jack Kerouac School of Disembodied Poetics*, playing his guitar and leading chants during some of the poetry reading and meditation sessions.

He wouldn't be in Boulder this summer because his wife was expecting their baby any day now. For certain he would not be there until late summer and only if Lama Tinley requested so. Or so he said. We talked until conversation wore thin.

Two weeks later my ride and camping adventure from Taos to Boulder dropped me off on Broadway near the University of Colorado campus. I was grateful, but our time spent had run its course.

I was left standing at the intersection pondering which way to find the Naropa office where I had been promised a note would be tacked on the billboard with contact information to rendezvous with Gainesville friend Crazy Rick Mumford.

In my reverie, an old yellow Mercedes sedan with a mandala sticker on the rear window pulled alongside. Rolling down the passenger window, Bhagavan Das leaned across his female passenger and said: "Walk down the street two blocks. The Dharma Center will be on your left."

Surprised and perplexed I responded, "I thought you weren't coming this summer."

"I'm not," he said and drove away.

And I never saw David Padwa at his mountain home in Taos. It wasn't until weeks later that I met Lama Tinley, sitting lotus position on a riverbank in long flowing robes, as I drifted slowly by in an inner tube.

Serendipity is, by definition, peculiar. People and circumstances converge in an unlikely manner, unplanned and highly unpredictable. Like vibrations of a butterfly's wings on

the wind, we can opt to receive what we cannot rationally understand or intellectually accept.

To do so, we must be willing to surrender to the moment,
swept into the sound of one hand clapping.

We encounter certain people at intervals in our lives for a
reason. Some are understandably binding. Other paths cross,
and then fade into timelessness, only later to resurface, and
underscore meaning for what once we thought to be ephemeral.

You can't control the waves, but you can learn how to surf.
- Swami Satchidananda's mantra on life.

An average day of overhead waves rolling into Puerto Escondido, Mexico. I lived there on and off, drawn by its world-class surf and vibrant spirit.

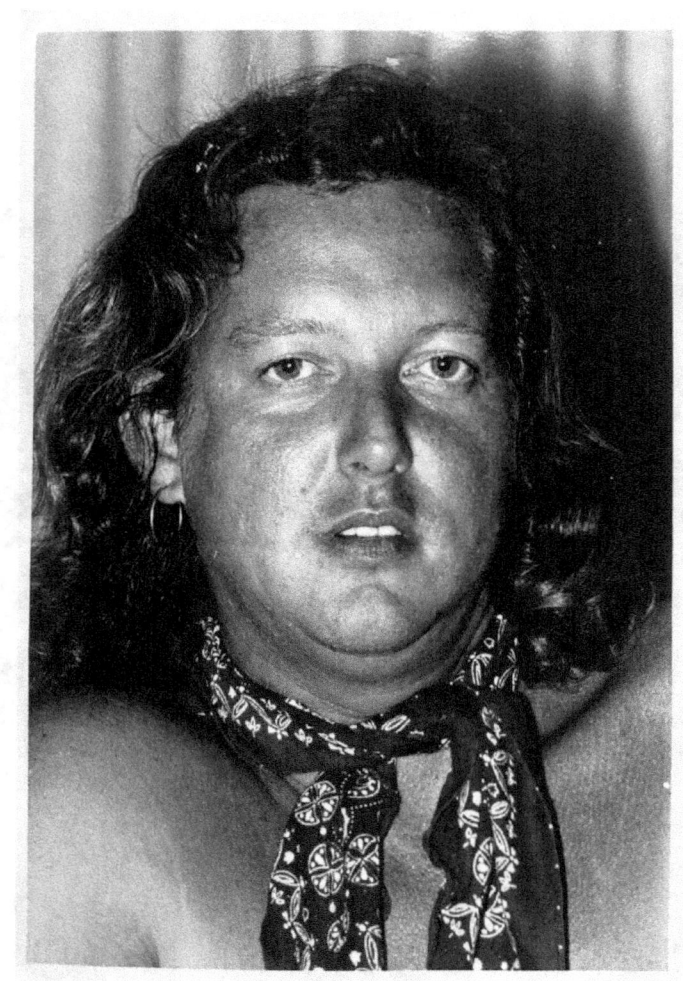

And I can't wait to get on the road again.

TAOS HERE I COME

"I was growing older but not up."
— from the Captain's Log

Francois pulled the car over for me to unload my backpack and guitar. The road from Santa Fe to Taos lay ahead.

Like any doting mother, she couldn't quite grasp why I would abandon a new car for my thumb.

"Doesn't make much sense," she said. "It's 400 miles to Boulder, and the roads going over the Continental Divide are still iced over."

"You're a writer," I reminded my new friend. "I need the experience. Never hitchhiked growing up. Not that I'm 'grown up.' Don't want to be. Never plan on it. No future in losing the innocence of a child at play."

She laughed nervously, shook her head in playful frustration, told me to be careful, then turned the car around and headed back toward Santa Fe.

There I was at age 32, growing older but not up, standing on the dusty roadside with my thumb out, pointing north. Not much traffic in the New Mexico desert, I thought. Several cars sped onward.

I looked like a bohemian poster boy: shoulder-length hair, bandana, and corduroy jeans with an embroidered butterfly on one knee, white blouse shirt, guitar and backpack.

On the road, I allowed myself a full-faced grin to the late spring sun, gnats circling my head. I drifted into a brief reverie, thinking about how I felt standing alone on the roadside, so many miles from family and friends.

A free spirit on the loose, like others I had read about who chose a similar path to discover just what life is supposed to be about, knowing the only way to truly find out is to face oneself head-on.

My path was vicarious, voluntary not obligatory, yet soul-seeking. A pilgrimage to the mecca of Beat writers gathering soon in Boulder.

In my fantasy, I was about to applaud all pioneers of the free spirit who had preceded me as the truck slid to a stop and interrupted my mental meanderings.

"Hey buddy, where you heading?" the old timer yelled.

I had gathered my pack and guitar and walked briskly to his pickup.

"Taos," I said.

"I can take you about 25 miles if that helps," he said.

What the hell, I thought. Might as well get started. Going nowhere standing here.

The next ride took me into Taos as the sun was going down. I walked into the nearest bar filled with cowboys coming and going like women at a bake sale. Turned out they were on the trail of cattle rustlers, modern day thieves who had been loading cows into trailers and carrying them off to market.

Like all bartenders everywhere, as a stranger new in town, I got the whole story plus some of his rustling theories and point of view with my beer and directions to the nearest motel.

There was still enough daylight after checking in to grab my guitar case and head out across the town square, with its shrubbery, flowers and park benches. My eye went directly to a pretty, black-haired woman sitting alone, reading *Zen and the Art of Motorcycle Maintenance.*

I stopped in front of her, opened my guitar case, and pulled out my copy of Pirsig's book.

"One of two books I brought from Florida," I said, opening the conversation.

"What's the other?" she questioned.

"Patanjali's Sutras," I said.

She knew the book, unusual considering its esoteric standing.

"You on some kind of spiritual quest?" she asked, her eyes dancing a mischievous minuet. "Sort of," I replied, surprised at her obvious intelligence and charm. "Would you like to join me for a spiritual beer?"

At that precise moment her traveling companion Peter walked up. We were politely introduced and exchanged stories.

Turned out he was finishing his doctorate at the University of Washington on poet Theodore Roethke. She lived in a brownstone in the most exclusive section of Georgetown. They had met at a think tank in Princeton, New Jersey, and were on the road themselves, getting romantically acquainted, camping in canyons, heading to Aspen.

Serendipity was scattering its semen everywhere. We were instant companions excitedly sharing graduate school dramas and talking poetry and music.

They had arrived only an hour earlier. Peter was checking out hotel rooms while she waited in the park. I pointed across the square to my place, espousing its charm and historic claims.

Then we all walked over so they could get a villa, and afterward ventured to the closest bar, said to have live music.

Peter also played the guitar, sang, and wrote lyrics. We ordered drinks, brazenly told the bartender how much better performers we were than was humanly possible, and conceded to get on stage.

How things magically happen gets right down weird if you put too much emphasis on the analysis. Often, we "think" too much and miss an opportunity that seems too good to be true. Perhaps we feel we don't deserve divine gifts. Maybe we never knew they exist.

Stars do fall from the sky. Angels dance on pinheads. We are all one in this dance of life.

As the memorable day and evening reached their zenith, we said our goodnights and happily went to our respective rooms. The pact had been made, I would join them on our mutual journey, sleeping in canyons, crossing the Rockies to Aspen, and ultimately to Boulder.

My hitchhiking door had closed, another adventure opened.

First, they wanted to visit Santa Fe, where I had just come from. They invited me along, and I declined. Instead, gathering my guitar and journal, I walked to the Taos graveyard and found the tombstone of the infamous cowboy Kit Carson.

I always thought I was a cowboy in a past life. While my future travelling companions were visiting Santa Fe, I spent the day just us two, cowboys from different eras.

One in the ground, the other sitting in the dirt and scrabble of rock, graveside, searching for answers to life.

I was a dedicated cub scout until I discovered girls.

BOULDER BOUND
AND MORE SERENDIPITY

*"Just because I carried the gear
didn't mean I knew what I was doing."
— from the Captain's Log*

B oy Scouts never was my thing. Maybe I was
burned out from three years as a Cub Scout. My
blue uniform was so plastered in badges; I
should've earned a weightlifting badge just for wearing it.

Could have been the testosterone factor.

Changes in hormones, changes in attitude.

Once out of blue and into the drab green Boy Scout uniform, I lost interest.

My badge of choice became girls.

After a year as a "tenderfoot," I was given an ultimatum:
go camping now and earn your "second class" badge or turn
in your uniform.

I packed my sleeping bag and matches without
much enthusiasm.

The night before we were to leave, my next-door neighbor
called to say her two nieces from Augusta were coming to visit
for the weekend.

So much for sleeping outdoors on the hard ground with a
bunch of guys.

I never looked back.

So it shouldn't come as a surprise that, on our first camping night, we set the canyon on fire. It wasn't exactly a blazing inferno, but we all smelled like charred wood for the next week. Just one of those things.

That's why they call them accidents.

We had a few more camping incidents en route to Boulder, like me picking an inappropriate campsite in pitch-black darkness on the outskirts of Aspen.

We had been driving all day, after crossing the still-frozen and treacherous Continental Divide at night, as soon as they opened the road for travel, and we were exhausted.

Like three Saturn missiles, we shot upright in the pre-dawn hours when a tractor-trailer came roaring past just feet from our heads.

Peter bordered on being angry. "I thought you were an experienced camper," he yelled. "You almost got us killed!"

Just because I carried a fashion-statement Kelty backpack and trendy North Face sleeping bag doesn't make up for lack of experience *(Made me a professional camper, I thought)*.

"I got kicked out of Boy Scouts," I confessed. "You see, there was this girl next door..." I began to explain as they loaded their gear and started the engine.

As fast as Peter drove that day, I got the impression they wanted to get rid of me.

In fact, when we reached Boulder, they pulled up to the nearest curb and drove off before my door was totally closed.

C'est la vie! That's how things happen.

One door closes and another opens.

I captained a 60-ft schooner "Bright Star" for a year
in Tortola, British Virgin Islands.
L–R: my son Trey, second wife Anita,
daughter Kim, and her husband Richard.

ON THE ROAD AGAIN

*"My mission was self-discovery. Sometimes focus requires
time alone to ponder and reflect and allow
serendipity to enter the equation."*
— from the Captain's Log

Six weeks later, I was on the road again.

This time with writer Lewis McAdams. We met at the *Jack Kerouac School of Disembodied Poetics* and made a pact.

Both of us were heading to California.

Coincidentally enough, he was leaving his wife and two kids behind to join environmental activist Peter Warshall and his girlfriend, poet Joann Kyger, at Peter's home in Bolinas, a very laid-back, progressive village in Marin County, north of San Francisco.

Lewis needed a getaway place where he could write.

Like my Florida separation experience, Lewis's wife also pulled the plug on his planned transportation. We decided to both post bulletin board notices around town and put the word out about our intention to reach the West Coast.

We would be a package deal.

I got the call. Tricia was a grammar schoolteacher winding down classes. She wanted someone to share travel expenses and driving.

On summer break, she was packing reading material for a six-week trek with her English sheepdog, Bali, heading north from San Francisco with no specific destination or itinerary, just a general game plan to reach the Oregon coast.

The year before, she went south all the way down the Baja.
She would pick me up first, then Lewis.

I was miserable.

On my hike up the path through the woods to the headwaters of Boulder Creek, for an inner tube ride that terminated in downtown, I brushed bare-chested against poison oak.

Calamine lotion doesn't work.

Itching goes from an unpleasant stage to one that borders on pain.

Scratching only opens sores, spreading the rash.

I later learned that poison oak and ivy enter the bloodstream and take about nine days to run its course.

A friend, the night before, mixed a poultice meant to ease discomfort.

As it dried, I left a trail of disgusting green globs in my wake.

I was not looking forward to the 24-hour-plus drive across country, especially when Tricia pulled up to the driveway in her 1967 VW bug, just like the one I had back home.

The back seat had been removed for Bali's creature comfort.

One of us would ride in back with luggage and her 100-pound ball of living fur. The other up front.

I loaded my backpack and guitar, and we headed for Lewis' house.

He was standing roadside with his suitcase and typewriter, his two kids clinging to his legs, and his wife tears running down her cheeks.

For me, the scene was uncomfortably déjà vu.

We all felt awkward as Lewis quickly squeezed luggage into the back with me and my new fuzzy buddy, Bali, then climbed into the passenger seat with the typewriter on his lap.

My plan was to head south from San Francisco to Santa Cruz and rendezvous with William Burroughs, Jr., even though we had never met, and he didn't know of my planned arrival.

I just thought it appropriate, since he had roomed the year before with my professor friend.

Burroughs' Sr. warned, "They may have run him out of town before you get there."

I would take my chances.

Eleven years later, in 1986, I would reflect on this venture.

Having earned my captain's license while living on my sailboat and teaching college, I fled the teaching bureaucracy in Miami and was hired as captain of a 60-foot schooner in Tortola, capital of the British Virgin Islands.

One particular charter brought a retired Air Force military officer, his wife, son and daughter-in-law.

In our briefing before setting sail, the old man, his life accustomed to regimen and giving orders, produced an itinerary for the week.

Each minute accounted for in military time.

All eyes were on me as I read his schedule, smiled at everyone, then tore the schedule several times for emphasis.

"Whichever way the wind blows," I simply explained.

I was on the road again.

First time west of the Mississippi. Looking for answers to questions that wake us at night in terror.

There has to be something more profound to this life than mundane jobs, economic hassles, tired bodies, ticky-tacky houses, car payments, insurance policies, television, fast food, fat bodies, dysfunctional families, lousy sex, sickness and death.

Just as there has to be more meaning than mansions, power, private planes, fat-riddled cuisine, miserable marriages, high fashion, face lifts, belly tucks, sickness and death.

It's not about what you've got, how much, or whom you know.

Others may not agree. Certainly, millions adopt the above criteria as their lifestyle. Free will. We all have choice.

Personally, I refuse to settle for less than aliveness. I want to know I have lived life to its fullest when time comes to leave. I long to understand more than what I have been told to accept without any merit. Mediocrity makes me cringe.

So does complacency and excuses for not being alive.

Maybe I'm just an eternal optimist. Certainly, I've been branded a dreamer on frequent occasion. Not to mention romantic. Or crazy Zen lunatic.

I want to know what this experience is supposed to be about other than a transitory coming and going.

For me, this journey on the road had more to do with going home than running away from it. We must first find out who we are before we can be ourselves.

Twenty-four hours later we were crossing the Golden Gate Bridge, past lovely and expensive Sausalito, up coastal Pacific Highway One and into Bolinas – more a village than a town. We found Peter Warshall's house. No one was there.

Lewis unloaded his gear. We were standing on the dirt road when Peter came sauntering up with his galvanized bucket filled with goat's milk.

My itching had gotten worse; blisters having spread to my abdomen. Itching, like tickling, gets painful. I knew what I needed to ease discomfort. Topical cortisone ointment.

The solution is simple.

Stop itching, no more scratching, blisters don't pop, nothing spreads.

Only you can't walk into a drugstore, tell them what you need, show them the obvious, and get an ointment just strong enough to work. That's because the medical establishment has closed doors on common sense. You must see a doctor and get a prescription for simple solutions to basic problems.

I would wait it out.

Road weary and psyched to be on the west coast, Tricia and I said our goodbyes to Lewis.

Tricia's game plan was to head north, mine south. Before parting company, we decided on San Francisco, and headed for the art district of North Beach.

We tied Bali's makeshift rope leash to a light pole outside the bar famous for down and out musicians and poets who gathered nightly to jam and jabber.

Pat O'Sullivan was sitting at the bar sucking down cheap draft. Ferlinghetti's City Lights Press, just up the hill from the bar, had published several of his books.

An old adage crossed my mind. The apple really doesn't fall too far from the tree.

This was Patty's home away from home. Actually, it was more home than where he lived, around the corner in a five-dollar-a-night flophouse.

A tiger, he explained, spewing spittle into my face, chewed off his missing arm when he was with the circus.

Another down-and-out City Lights poet, Bob Kaufman, was dancing around the jukebox in his red kimono when the music stopped. This was his primary residence too. He asked for my assistance, having trouble focusing on the coin slot.

So went the night. One of Ray Charles' former band members joined the group of musicians gathering on stage in the back room. He had a crash and burn story, a refrain familiar with most of the group.

Drugs, divorce, car wrecks, lost jobs, penniless... one thing they had in common was music. This was their life, and they gathered at this spot to lose themselves in what talent remained.

Back on the street, Bali's rope leash was dangling on the lamp post. She had chewed it in half and was off on her own romp in North Beach.

We found her entertaining some locals a half block away, the other half of her leash dangling from her neck.

We had driven non-stop, Denver to San Francisco to Bolinas and back to San Francisco, on the road and in the bars for 36 hours.

We got in the VW bug and headed back across the bridge to Sausalito, then up the hill to Muir Woods, overlooking San Francisco Bay. Parking in the scenic view overlook, we grabbed our sleeping bags, walked into the woods, and set up camp under a large eucalyptus tree.

Thick morning fog dripping on my face came at sunrise. Our sleeping bags were soaked. Time to be on our way.

Loud music greeted us as we neared the parking area. A white Cadillac convertible, its top down, and a partially naked couple making love in the back seat, was the occasion for early morning rock and roll.

Welcome to California, I thought, just like in the movies.

Tricia dropped me off at the ferry landing in Sausalito. I had her watch my belongings long enough for me to visit the nearby drugstore and plead to no avail for medication to relieve my poison oak, continuing to spread over my tormented body.

It was nice having a traveling companion, she asked if I wanted to change my mind and go north.

Being with someone else is always tempting, even if for the wrong reasons.

With considerable reluctance, I rejected her offer, knowing I needed time and space.

My mission was self-discovery.

Sometimes, focus requires time alone to ponder and reflect and allow serendipity to enter the equation.

We must be willing to stand in our aloneness and surrender fully for this to occur.

This much I had already learned.

I watched her yellow VW drive away with mixed feelings.

Old emotions of holding on gripped my chest.

We find our truths at the heart center.

Dropping coins into the pay phone, I dialed my wife 3,000 miles back in Florida. The sadness and uncertainty on both ends of the conversation were pervasive.

As I hung up, the ferry pulled into the landing.

A certain irony crept into my longing as we cruised past Alcatraz, the long-abandoned prison where escape was considered impossible. A few were thought to have made it off the "rock." No one knows for certain.

In the distance loomed San Francisco, a city of romance and adventure. We would dock at Fisherman's Wharf, a tourist destination for food and consumerism.

I hoisted my backpack, grabbed the guitar case handle, and started walking up the long hill towards City Lights Bookstore, cloaked in a melancholia, pondering if any of us ever find freedom.

My dad showing off his "Big Catch."

WELCOME TO SAN FRANCISCO

"I now knew more about these choices than before I had arrived."
— from the Captain's Log

Across from City Lights Bookstore was a questionable hotel along a street of mostly hard-core porn shops and topless joints. Burly, unshaven T-Shirted management hung in doorways hawking passersby.

Funds were running low. No time for the kind of discretion I was taught back south in my youth.

This was another kind of cotillion.

The word "hotel" barely fit the narrow sidewalk doorway that led up a long stairway to a lobby with a television on its last leg. Half the vertical screen had blackened, so you only got a picture from the waist down.

A group of grizzled and smelly men with blank expressions sat around the tube as if it were the final World Series game. No one seemed to care or notice that half the frame was missing.

It reminded me of a visit I once took with my psychology class in high school to the state mental hospital. I decided then not to become a psychiatrist.

Hidden partially behind a barred window, the desk clerk absently slid back two dollars change from my ten.

The price was right, the place wasn't.

A shared bathroom was at the end of the hallway. My room had a bed, washbasin in the corner, Gideon Bible, and a window looking out on a roof with empty liquor bottles and human feces, where hotel guests had climbed out the window instead of using the hallway toilet.

During my two-night stay, I never pulled back the bed covers to see what might be lurking beneath the soiled spread. I slept in my clothes, on my back, protecting my wallet, with one arm draped around the guitar.

Sleep didn't come easy in San Francisco, with music pounding above the shouts of drunken patrons into the wee hours from the topless clubs.

Perhaps it was my upbringing that brought out the paranoia. No one ever messed with my belongings, or me.

I stayed in the room only long enough to rest, if you could call it that, leaving my guitar and backpack while exploring the art district.

Weaving my way into a tight-knit inner circle of late-night workers, mostly bartenders and waitresses, we made the club rounds together, meeting characters and crazies, stopping in alleyways to share a joint.

Most of them I'll never remember. Some I won't forget.

Maybe the names have vanished, but situations of life are indelible.

We were on the streets one night when this attractive woman, bruised and battered, pleaded for help. Her face was purpled and swollen. She was someone they all knew. For some reason, she focused on me. My entire body quivered with outrage.

Then her husband showed up, pissed at her complaining.

Our eyes still connected, he picked up on our energy.

So did the others, my newfound friends.

I was pulled aside. Mark said this is how it is. Nothing I could do. They had all tried.

Suddenly I flashed back to age twelve.

My dad had been transferred to Memphis, Tennessee.

We were on the road, driving through the mountains, when traffic slowed. A head-on collision had occurred only minutes before. Cars had already pulled over to help.

As we crawled by the carnage, a young man lay on the ground covered in blood. I looked into his dying eyes, pleading for help. I begged my father to stop, to do something, anything, to relieve the misery.

My dad was a good man. He believed in everything righteous. Having grown up during the depression on a farm, he knew struggle. He and his brothers hunted squirrels and rabbits for dinner when food was scarce.

They taught me. I never liked the killing, only the hunt. A basic primal instinct, now outdated, in the name of sport.

A young man lay in the grass on the roadside, dying. I witnessed helplessness of death in his pleading eyes. "So why," I asked, "can't we stop and make him better, save his life?"

We drove on. Dad knew there was nothing he could do. He lacked medical training. Others were already on the scene giving aid.

For most of my adulthood I have clutched the steering wheel driving highways. I'm actually skilled and have a fondness for sports cars as adrenaline machines. Still, I would rather not drive.

I'll never forget those dying eyes and plea for help.

More importantly, I've learned not to judge.

This has eased my tension on the highway. Dad's reasons for continuing were probably multiple, not the least to spare family the gory and inevitable.

Early the next morning, after another restless night in San Francisco, I walked past the barred desk clerk's habitat, a television with its partial test pattern droning in the empty lobby, and out onto Columbus Street.

The air was cool and damp. I was wearing my favorite suede jacket, the only one I brought for my journey. My mind was relegated to understanding why we do the things we do and live to celebrate or regret our choices.

I now knew more about these choices than before I had arrived. I also had a painful lesson in being non-judgmental.

It was a great city bus ride across town to the Pacific Highway. My thumb extended, I was on the road heading south. Destination: Santa Cruz.

Worst damn case of poison ivy I've ever had.

POISON IVY, POT,
AND THE VD CLINIC

"You either can or you can't. You live and then you die."
— from the Captain's Log

The red, neon flashing Lyn-Del Motel sign outside my window was distracting enough, but night brought little sleep as the poison ivy upped its amperage.

Daylight couldn't come soon enough.

To hell with my limited budget, I decided, looking bleary-eyed through Santa Cruz's yellow pages for a dermatologist. He was out of town until the following week.

California is known for its free "people's clinic." No listing. I tried the County Health Department. Sorry. The only free clinic we have is the VD clinic at the county hospital.

"But I've got poison ivy," I explained.

"We can't help you then.

You need to make a doctor's appointment."

I itched and hurt all over. If you've never had poison ivy, you can't imagine the torment. The itch goes way below the skin's surface.

Once in high school, I got it on my feet working in the flowerbed. My feet were so swollen I couldn't wear socks, not to mention the thought of shoes.

Night times are worse for some reason.

A repeat of the night before, I would drift off to restless sleep and awaken, my body rubbing the sheets seeking relief.

Enough was enough. I would try anything. It took two bus transfers to the hospital. My logic was, if I got to the VD clinic, they would treat my poison ivy.

Several receptionists were busy shuffling papers in the hospital lobby teeming with people coming and going.

"Excuse me," I whispered,

"Could you direct me to the VD clinic?"

"OH, THE VD CLINIC," the receptionist shouted, loud enough for anyone standing outside on the street to hear.

"TAKE A NUMBER AND HAVE A SEAT OVER THERE," she bellowed, pointing to four couches filled with mostly young people all staring in my direction.

The number hung on a peg like you would find in a luncheonette. I grabbed number 12 and wandered red-faced to an open space on the couch. Turns out, they were ALL here for the same thing: the VD clinic.

I'm not naïve, but neither have I had venereal disease, not that it couldn't have easily happened. From looking at these attractive and unfortunate recipients, I guess I had been damn lucky. You would never know just by looks.

An hour passed before my number was called.

"Number 12," chirped the woman with a clipboard in a white coat.

"Follow me."

She led me down the hallway to a small office, not bothering to close the door. She was all business. I got the impression she didn't care much for her job. Maybe she had a prejudice against sexually transmitted diseases.

Whatever, she had the personality of Attila the Hun.

"Name," she demanded, followed by age, address, and the usual data for the records.

She never once looked me in the eyes, just focused on the sheet of paper on which she was writing on.

"Symptoms," she demanded.

"Well," I began, "it started on my chest, spread down to my waist, around to my back, and down to my pubic area."

She was writing furiously.

"Worse case of poison ivy I've ever had in my life."

She abruptly stopped writing and, for the first time, looked me in the eyes with a menacing glare.

"This is a VD clinic," she glowered.

"I know," I pleaded, "but I don't have much money and there are no people's clinics here in Santa Cruz and the dermatologist is out of town, so I thought if I came here, someone could prescribe some cortisone..."

My voice trailed off. Without further comment, she got up from her desk.

I heard her shrill voice down the hallway: "Number 13."

I was still seated when she came back into the office and pointed for the next client to take a chair.

"Name," she began.

It was as if I didn't even exist.

Rising, I walked back through the lobby, out the door, and into the cool Santa Cruz midday, waiting for the bus to arrive.

That night I slept like a baby. No more pain or itching. I later learned that poison ivy takes a tour through the bloodstream, lasting about nine days. My time was up.

The next day, a group of fun-loving, out-of-town community college students checked in next door. They were boisterously enjoying a last fling before school resumed.

I was sitting outside in my jeans, Buddha shirt, and sandalwood beads, drinking a beer and playing the guitar, when they arrived.

From the second-floor porch, you could look down the street two blocks and see Monterey Bay.

If I can't be on the water, I at least want to see it.

The drinking age in California was 21, but where there's a will, there's a way. They had a source back home, so they brought up a case of beer and began the party.

One of the girls had mixed some pills with her alcohol and took a nasty spill off her skateboard down a steep hill.

She was bruised and bloody when they scraped her off the street and asked for my assistance, being that I was an older guy, presumably knowledgeable about these kinds of things.

We spent the next two hours picking pebbles out of her body and dousing her in hydrogen peroxide. No bones were sticking through her skin, so I pronounced her well.

By then I had gained their confidence enough to be offered a joint that I readily accepted. By late afternoon we were all stoned, playing the guitar and singing.

They thought I was cool, and I found them fun.

I've never thought much of the age factor. Even when my kids were small and asked questions, I always gave them an answer, even if it was an adult-sized reply. It always satisfied.

I also did outrageously playful things, encouraging the expansion of joyful horizons. Lack of imagination is our primary limitation in life.

"Ageism," like communism, capitalism, and any other "ism," can categorize individuals into some group identity that doesn't necessarily fit.

This belief probably came from my grandmother, who was loved by everyone and always lied about her age. Up until she turned 100, she said she was much younger. Once she hit the century mark, she would exaggerate on the high end.

I never tell my age. It limits you. If pressed, I will most often pick a number at random. Sometimes I forget. The chronology usually doesn't fit.

What's the big deal, anyway? You either can or you can't. You live, and then you die.

So in many respects, and also due to my openness and willingness to buy them beer, I became one of the gang. That's when we organized the "Santa Cruz Pot Brigade."

Seems they had been storing pot seeds in a jumbo-sized zip lock, enough to start a very large marijuana plantation. My advice was solicited on the eve of their return home. One last night, one final fling.

They needed two cases of beer, munchies, and a celebratory game plan.

"Got it," I said. "Johnny Appleseed."

"Who is he?" they asked.

I thought everyone knew the Johnny Appleseed story.

"He went around the countryside planting apple tree seeds," I continued.

"We don't have apple seeds, but we do have pot seeds."

We adopted a slogan:

"A pot plant in every yard."

The idea was contagious.

At midnight, armed with jugs of water, spoons, and seeds, we set out into the neighborhoods of Santa Cruz, moving house to house, using the spoons to dig holes to plant seeds among the flower beds.

It took nearly two hours to empty the zip lock and re-turn to the motel, mission accomplished.

The next day they left to resume their life's journey.

I had been in Santa Cruz for two weeks. No sign of William Burroughs' Jr. Like his dad warned, he had been run out of town. And I was running out of money.

Dry cleaning is not for everyone.

HUSTLING LAUNDRY

"My karma is immediate."
— from the Captain's Log

H ustling laundry curbside was probably my first real full-time summer job. Days were long, and pay was low.

Mostly I ran, trying to keep up with people dropping off dry cleaning and laundry on the way to work in the mornings and picking up late afternoon fresh bundles en route to home.

I'd bundle and wrap string around the drop offs, put their name on a slip of paper, slide it under the string, and toss it in a basket. A truck would pick up dry cleaning after the morning rush and take it downstairs for cleaning.

Afternoons I would load washable bundles in the machines. Mrs. Johnson was an older woman who managed the service. Mostly she took money, made change, and told me what to do.

I was 14, and for as long as I could remember, which couldn't have been long since I was only 14, I had saved to buy a car.

My 11-hour workdays would purchase new tires and insurance for the 1947 Dodge Coupe for which I paid $137.50. I was the proud fourth owner.

I insisted on paying my own way. Independent and self-reliant, I wanted to do it myself.

One day I spaced out and forgot to get anybody's name to go with his or her laundry.

The cleaning truck made its usual rounds.

When the dry cleaning came back the next day, there was no identification.

Unfortunately, the big boss happened to stop by the store when the first customer arrived, and we began the arduous task of matching unmarked parcels with the owners.

Seemed every time something went wrong, he would show up precisely at the moment of discovery. It was uncanny.

The law of karma is much like cause and effect. When we do something good, something good happens. And vice-versa.

If we are living consciously and purposefully striving to be truthful and evolve as human beings, the faster the return.

My karma is immediate. I say something bordering on negative about someone, they suddenly appear – leaving me to wonder whether they heard my commentary.

I take something that really doesn't belong to me, and then I get overcharged on my very next purchase or lose something special.

I've gotten to be very, very careful. I refrain even from killing insects. If they are here, they must serve a purpose. Everything in its place.

I used to not pay such close attention. My awareness factor was considerably lower in my early days.

One of my jobs was to mop the floor. During a lull one day, I turned on the faucet to fill the bucket. The faucet was in a rather unusual location near the rear of the store in a cubbyhole.

All of a sudden, we got busy outside.

Back and forth I raced.

The boss showed up and we both splashed inside the store together. "What the hell happened here?!" he screamed.

The front of the store was slightly elevated. Back at the still-running faucet, the water stood a foot deep.

Water had backed up into lower bins holding freshly done laundry. He was too flustered to talk right. Everything he spewed sounded like Pig Latin.

I was sent down to the grocery for brooms to sweep out the water.

I thought the entire scene comical and developed a laughing case that wouldn't stop, tears streaming from my eyes, doubled over, my stomach aching.

"Go get the brooms NOW," the boss yelled, spittle running down his now bright red face.

I was still laughing when I walked back in the front door. Now the boss' face was stroke crimson.

In his right hand he was waving a poster we usually kept in the front window of the fall high school football schedule.

Unfortunately, with the water rising to the front door, the boss man had picked up the schedule. On the backside I had sketched an unflattering caricature of him.

I was still laughing when he raised his broom above his head and I ran from the cleaners, jumped in my car, and headed home for some R&R until school resumed.

My car had new tires and insurance.

I took it to the cleaners so to speak.

The job was history now.

Summer was coming to an end anyway.

The end of a day.

RADIO DJ AND CYANIDE

"Some jobs make you sick. Some call you forward.
Know the difference."
— from the Captain's Log

Some jobs really suck. You get to hate them so much that the loathing turns pathological. Then you just can't do it anymore.

This is a good thing, a warning, and a primal call to change. Shifting gears scares most people.

Usually change involves risk taking. Some people simply never learn to listen. They get ulcers instead. Or fall down the stairs. Lousy health or workman's comp becomes an escape hatch.

The warning bell went off working while working in layaway at J.C. Penney's. I hustled packages back in the dusty basement bowels, a labyrinth of overhead heating and air conditioning ducts, on weekends and holidays.

Two sweet old blue heads worked the front desk. The environment was dingy and dirty.

One day I couldn't take it anymore. I became nauseous. Dad came to pick me up. What we didn't know then, I know now. My mind and body and spirit were rebelling, directing me away from a dead-end toxic situation.

There was no turning back. Once we get the message, we've got it. You can't give it back. Call it inner voice, intuition, universal wisdom, or just plain common sense, call it any name that suits your fancy, it still exists.

I didn't understand it then, but I was learning four of life's great lessons. Show up, pay attention, tell the truth, and don't be attached to the outcome.

I was somewhere where I wasn't supposed to be for whatever reason, so I moved on. One of my big lessons that moment was not to be in retail business. Claustrophobic and unchallenging, I desired excitement and frequent stimulation of the senses.

Columbia, South Carolina didn't have much to offer a teenager as a stimulus package for mind expansion.

Digging for clues, I chose radio as my venue to pursue. I brazenly walked into the most popular Top 40 station, requesting an audience with the station manager.

George Buck was blind as a bat. The receptionist warned me not to offer a handshake as she led me to his office.

He would never see it. Buck, wearing coke bottle eyeglasses, thought I was there for career information. I wanted a job... NOW. Summer was just around the corner.

An hour later, when he offered his hand welcoming me to WCOS Radio, 1400 on your radio dial, I shook it vigorously, eager and grateful. My homework had paid off in spades.

Listening to his competitor's drive time morning broadcasts, I realized no one had updated local news. It was all regurgitated from the newspaper.

My proposal was simple. I would check with police, fire, and highway patrol at the crack of dawn and write breaking news for the 8 a.m. talk show. Buck was impressed. He would give me a shot at minimum wage.

I was out of retail and into entertainment. Not bad considering I had no prior writing or radio experience.

I pushed for more, hungry to get airtime.

I filed records, then set up Sunday morning church remotes, sitting in a back room at a different church every week with a portable control board adjusting sound levels. The control board was patched into a phone line. That's the way it worked.

What they didn't know, and never found out, was that during the sermon I would get in my car, drive to Taylor Street Pharmacy, buy a fountain Coke and cheese crackers, and return to my post, snack in hand.

My big break came at 11 p.m. one Saturday night when DJ Dan Moon got called up by the military reserves. He hosted a midnight-to-daybreak request show live above Doug Broom's Drive-In restaurant on Main Street. Unable to find another announcer, the station owner called me.

Buck was obviously desperate.

"Think you can do it?" he asked.

"No problem," I said, trembling as I drove downtown, took the stairs to the rooftop, and climbed a stepladder into my glass tower for my first night emceeing the "All Night Satellite."

More all-night gigs followed during my senior year of high school. I continued writing morning news.

One fall morning, a break came.

A call came into the detective's office at the Columbia Police Department while I was browsing the nightly offense reports. A body had reportedly been found on the University of South Carolina campus lawn, almost directly across from the radio station.

Only several miles from the police station, I arrived before the police. Thinking at first the detectives were pulling a gag, I was turning to leave when I saw the body lying face up in the grass about ten feet from where I was standing.

I walked over and looked down. He was a teenager, and his lips had turned purple.

Several minutes passed before I heard a police officer yell, "Hey, what do you think you're doing?"

What do you say you're doing when you're standing over a dead body? I thought.

"I work for WCOS Radio News," I said. "The call came in while I was reading the offense reports."

"You aren't going to announce this on the air, are you?" he asked apprehensively. "Every mother in the state will be in a panic if you do."

"Tell you what," I said. "I won't air anything if you let me go on the investigation, keep me posted, and let me be the first with the story."

We had a deal. I got my story.

It was not a happy one.

Suicide seldom is.

He was a high school student who took cyanide poison obtained from the lab where his father worked as a professor.

Sometimes no news is good news.

Captain Madness interviews Special Forces and joins night maneuvers on the Indian River Lagoon outside Melbourne, FL.

TEENAGE MARRIAGE
AND THE KKK

"Enthusiasm and tenacity can go a long way."
— from the Captain's Log

A year later I married a high school student who lived around the corner from my grandparents. I was 18; she was three weeks shy of 16.

We were young, in lust and in love, in that order.

Sex trumps common sense and has caused the ruin of many since the beginning of time.

We were, as time proved, extremely naive, stubborn and stupid.

After all, rock and roll singer Jerry Lee Lewis was 22 when he married his 13-year-old first cousin once removed

Young marriages weren't uncommon in the South during the sixties. But the Vietnam War and a more mature shift in consciousness changed all that.

But it makes for a romantic story, despite the long-term consequences, like divorce 18 years later, after the brain was finally fully developed (more or less anyway).

You could say this was a pretty good run for a young, harebrained decision.

An underage marriage was illegal back then in South Carolina, but you could cross the state line into Lincolnton, Georgia, and anything went.

A scrawny, bald-headed justice of the peace, Homer Legg (his real name), performed the brief ceremony in the courthouse, witnessed by a secretary and someone brought in off the street.

Still living with our parents, we had to cautiously plot our time together.

Her mother was wary of her daughter dating a college man.

October, and the state fair, provided the excuse, assisted by another young married couple who became our accomplices and even loaned us their bed to consummate the event.

We were what could appropriately be called "dirt poor" and didn't even have sufficient funds for the fair entrance fee. So I hopped a fence outside the 4-H cow and pig stalls, then pried the gate open enough for my newlywed to crawl through.

To further confirm our alibi, she called her mother from a phone booth with all the noise from carnival rides and said we had met some friends and asked if we could we stay out past the 9 p.m. time to be home.

We had just enough money for French fries and put down a quarter to gamble the mouse game where a mouse is released on a spinning wheel and runs into a hole of the winning number.

We won!

Number 13 and a stuffed red donkey, further confirming our fabrication.

I then took her home, where we kissed goodnight on the front porch, and I returned to my parents.

The next three weeks were what teen movies are made of.

A tenth-grade high school student, her father dropped her off at school and I would be parked nearby. Then we would go apartment hunting.

Since holidays were approaching, she found a part-time job at a department store.

I was a sophomore at the University of South Carolina and worked part-time at a local top 40 radio station writing news briefs for the early morning talk show.

We sneaked household items, like soap, and canned goods, and just about anything to set up housekeeping, out of our parents' larder and stored them in the trunk of my Ford Falcon.

Careful to maintain our secrecy, we rented a garage apartment from an owner who lived in another city. Life was simple in 1960, and not a lot of questions asked.

Anxious to start our lives together, and more importantly to make love in our bed rather than in the car or on my Dad's old army blanket on the 18th green at the Forest Lake Country Club golf course.

So one day we sat on a creek bank at Maxcy Gregg Park and composed passionate letters to each of our parents, pledging our love and determination to be together, threatening not to be seen again unless we had their word and consent to accept our marriage.

Sealing the envelopes, we put them in a suitcase in my bedroom. We had given instructions for my parents to meet at her parents at a prearranged time when we would call from a phone booth at the Exxon gas station within walking distance from our apartment.

Pledging one another to remain stalwart, knowing it would be an emotional encounter, we made the call. Then drove over to her parents, after receiving their promise not to interfere, for a most uncomfortable evening.

We had answers to everything.

"How are you going to live?"

Our response: "We have jobs."

"What kind of dump did you rent?"

We said: "A nice one bedroom, pine-paneled furnished apartment five minutes' drive."

"What about school?"

"We plan to finish."

Her mother asked, "I guess you've had sex?"

"Don't be ridiculous," the Dad responded.

"Of course they have."

After the interrogation, and nothing further to say, we left for home and marital bliss, learning the joys and tribulations of married life as they unfolded.

We were young and in love.

Now a journalism student at the University, I continued to work in radio part-time.

Although my skills were being honed, I deferred from my studies. Finally, the University "insisted" I take time off, placing me on academic suspension for a semester.

Needing a full-time job, I started applying at radio stations around the state.

There just weren't any openings for someone with limited experience, despite having worked in the largest market.

Mostly, there weren't any openings... period!

The job market was tight.

One day I filled out an application to drive a delivery truck and refill vending machines. My grandfather thought otherwise. He was the Comptroller for the State-Record newspaper and arranged a job interview with the city editor.

I entered the newsroom at the daily newspaper and introduced myself. The city editor remembered the campus suicide story and listened intently as I explained how I got my job at WCOS.

Enthusiasm and tenacity can go a long way.

He hired me on the spot, 30 days probation to see if I would work as a journalist, and assigned me a beat covering the library, post office, civic club speakers, and writing obits.

I charmed the librarian whose brother was a newspaper publisher, chased fires, turned bland Rotarian talks into human-interest fodder, and rightfully earned my keep as a full-fledged reporter.

A year later, having grossly over exaggerated my experience and abilities, I was hired at the Wilmington Star News in Wilmington, NC, as their primary reporter, covering city and county government. This was considered the most sensitive position for both accuracy and public relations.

Flying by the proverbial seat of my pants, I had never even had a civics class.

I crash-coursed politics, hanging dearly on every word, sensing the bullshit in the process and relying on intuition to guide me onward.

By the time my editors realized I had never attended a budget hearing, I had feigned enough to learn the right stuff.

There is a very fine line between authentic and hustling, curious or deceitful.

Truth-seeking becomes mulch for good intentions, producing right actions.

I moved on to the Raleigh News and Observer, rightfully now a political reporter, but cut my investigative teeth infiltrating the Ku Klux Klan.

Now I was having fun, snooping around parking lots at cross burnings, gathering license tag numbers, and dodging patrolling storm troopers in the process.

Trying to interview a Klansman at his home in the country, equipped with snarling junk-yard dogs, a yard filled with long-abandoned refrigerators, stoves, and rusting, derelict cars, I came face to face with an unwelcoming 12-gauge shotgun.

"I'm just trying to get your side of the story," I lobbied.

"If this shotgun don't get you, them dogs will," he said, waving the gun up and down my body, still seated in my shiny British racing red Austin Healey 3000.

I kept thinking that I might have made a mistake taking the top down, not because it would have helped against buckshot, but because the dogs growled at eye range.

Sometimes you just don't argue or run a bluff.

You lay down the cards and get the hell out of Dodge.

This was one of those times.

I didn't bother to turn the car around. I just hit reverse and backed several hundred yards, that seemed more like miles, out the dusty drive and onto the macadam.

Before it was all said and done, I had packed up my wife and daughter, sent them home to the parents, and changed my phone number.

This came the day after a rock with a warning note sailed through the huge plate-glass newspaper office front in downtown Raleigh.

Not too many years ago, I was reminded of that earlier event in my life when a personally threatening note was posted on the front door of Juno Beach City Hall in Florida.

Police took it seriously, paid me a visit, offering to patrol my home, and dusted the flyer for prints.

As a private citizen, I had taken on a cause against aggressive developers who were destroying the tiny town's environment.

They were slipping a zoning variance through the town council to allow high-density condos on environmentally sensitive property.

Insights gleaned as a reporter rose to the surface.

I recalled how scurrilous and unscrupulous local politicians could be when money is passed under the table for small favors.

Small favors always lead to larger ones.

Once started, there is no end.

Compromise becomes rationalization and then righteous indignation.

I had watched it happen in the smallest of North Carolina towns. Size was not a factor. Human nature, greed, power... these were the common denominators.

I took a stand, writing the facts on a flyer with the town council's group picture fashioned like a "wanted" poster for destroying the environment.

Knowing how the media likes to rationalize these days, I sent out a press release.

The Miami Herald, Palm Beach Post and Orlando Sentinel all called for quotes. Two television stations sent crews, pitting me against the establishment.

Locals packed city hall chambers.

I made an impassioned plea on behalf of the environment—quoting environmentalist Aldo Leopold and Henry David Thoreau.

I challenged the council to act responsibly in the interest of voters who had put them in office.

I received a standing ovation before the council granted unanimously to approve the variance.

The vote was predictable. That's why I left newspaper political reporting.

The system is mostly a sham.

You need to be constantly vigilant and informed.

Most people don't have or take the time for either.

So, we elect those to do it for us. Only human nature more often than not gets in the way.

And "human" wins out over "nature" most of the time.

Would-be Astro Ed Riley on the field for a week-long workout with the Astros.

TODAY'S SUNRISE

Fake it like a pro.

CLOWNS, BASEBALL,
AND APOLLO 17

*"Everybody has a story. We are all unique, one-of-a-kind
individuals. Our life on this planet is what we have in common."*
— from the Captain's Log

I've said it more than once: if you work as a journalist
four years, covering all angles, police beat to politics,
investigative to human interest, you gain more
insight into the human condition than most people garner
in their lifetime.

I put in seven years total.

The last two came after a hiatus to complete my bachelor's
degree and do a stint in advertising and public relations, iron-
ically helping would-be politicians get elected to office.

Pay was good. Satisfaction of having done something
meaningful and with purpose was skimpy. So, I returned to
journalism, this time with Gannett in Cocoa, Florida.

With my background, I got cream-puff assignments,
mostly writing feature stories for the Sunday supplement.

"Just average six stories a month," I was told, "and you
only need to stop by the office to pick up your paycheck."

Sometimes the editor had a specific story idea, but mostly
I was left on my own.

Now I was really free to explore my wanderlust and fantasies in the style made notable by writer George Plimpton.

Wondering how life would be as a clown, I performed one
night under the Ringling Bros. Big Top.

"You're a stupid clown," one spoiled kid told me as we paraded around the tent, up and down aisles, playing kazoos.

"You're a stupid kid," I shot back, leaving his stunned parents to sort out the beginnings of their son's potential delinquent behavior.

On the other hand, my delinquent behavior was fine-tuned. Besides, I was a clown for a night. I couldn't get fired.

Claustrophobia took on new meaning when they stuffed 17 clowns into one small car. You see it at every circus. The small vehicle with blackened windows comes careening center ring, doors fling open, and clown after clown emerges.

How it's done is simple and inhumane.

Seats are removed and clown upon clown stacked until the remaining clown is on top pressed between the roof and a car full of clowns. One wiggle causes a ripple effect, not to mention what happens if someone farts.

With my over-sized clown effect shoes, I was last one in, clown on top, shoes pressed against the windshield. If I wiggled, 16 clowns cursed.

Upping the ante, I contacted a professional baseball team, the Houston Astros, who spring train in Cocoa, Florida. Assuring them my athletic prowess would prevail; they sent a team of lawyers with liability papers in triplicate for me to sign.

"What position you wanna play?" the coaches asked.

"Wherever the ball comes least frequently," I replied.

"That'll be right field," Coach Fiercer said.

"Hey, you sure you played ball before?"

Actually, I made the Little League team for Family Finance my first tryout. I was 10. Being the youngest, I didn't get to see much action and quit mid-season out of boredom.

I played in Junior High. For half a season. Tall and lanky, they wouldn't let me pitch because you would lose too much weight during a game in the southern heat. Standing around third base waiting seemed like a waste of time.

It would be a long time coming before I could finally sit and meditate.

Mostly I played sandlot. Mays, a city park directly across the street from where I lived, was my sanctuary.

A quick peanut butter and jelly sandwich and glass of chocolate milk, and I was out the door, in the park until dark. We played softball, basketball, and tennis during prime season, each of us acting out our particular role model.

On cold rainy days we played ping-pong inside the park building. Other times we roller-skated in the concrete spray pool. Our large grassy front yard made for the best football field.

Always in motion, we honed our skills often, playing against larger and older neighborhood kids who belonged to this eclectic afternoon sporting menagerie.

I wrote stories about topless shoeshine girls, a black stripper named "Chocolate Delight," shylocks, Chubby Checker, and anybody or anything that caught my interest.

Everybody has a story. We are all unique, one-of-a-kind individuals. Our life on this planet is what we have in common.

Like the song by Sly and the Stones goes, "We are family."

I used this conviction to my advantage, ever the inquiring mind. Usually, it paid off.

Like old Ben Logan, a big guy on a longboard, who surfed Canaveral Pier every day regardless the weather, towing his heavy, outdated surfboard on a makeshift rig behind his bicycle from home several blocks inland.

Ben was sun-bleached and rugged. His love for surfing was admired by youngsters on new featherweight surfboards who watched from the beach on days they didn't consider waves challenging.

Turns out Ben was once a California highway patrolman who got discovered and played Tarzan in several movies. Now in his sixties, his passion became surfing.

Then there was the avid shark fisherman who hooked them from the end of the pier, climbed across the bait shop roof still managing his rod and reel, walked down the pier and would land his catch on the beach.

A neo-Nazi officer in the White People's Socialist Party out of Arlington, Virginia, he told me his story that got weird when I accepted a swig from his bottle of wine as I bonded with him one evening.

He had laced it with pills he would get by writing his own prescription.

Driving his mustang convertible heading to his grand-mother's up in Titusville where he was to show me his arsenal and seminal collection of Nazi memorabilia passed down by his deceased father, the "reds" kicked in, and the center line started wavering.

I pulled over to the roadside and let the effects subside.

My last formal assignment covered the last Apollo Mission, Flight 17, from a cruise ship anchored off Cape Canaveral.

Billed as "The Voyage Beyond Apollo," the SS Statendam cruise ship left from New York City. Academy scientists were on board to discuss what came next in space exploration.

Prominent science fiction writers on board included Isaac Asimov, Ben Bova, and Theodore Sturgeon.

So were Norman Mailer, Katherine Anne Porter, and a cadre of lesser-knowns.

Symposiums were scheduled during the sail to watch the last Apollo launch, then carry speakers, and paying passengers along with press to St. Thomas, then to Arecibo, Puerto Rico, home to the huge astronomical tracking center, and back to New York.

Only people weren't that interested.

All these luminaries and not enough passengers willing to pay the tariff. In a last-minute rush to salvage a potential disaster, the Holland cruise line, in a brazen public relations ploy, invited more media.

Focusing on the timely release of Norman Mailer's latest book on blonde bombshell Marilyn Monroe, they attracted fan and women's magazines otherwise uninterested in space travel.

Lack of consumer interest in the final Apollo hoop-de-rah-rah caught my attention, especially since I worked for the only newspaper sent into space.

That was the promotional brainstorm of Al Neuharth who used Cocoa Today newspaper as a launch pad, creating USA Today.

Young Jimmy Breslin, son of New York Herald Tribune columnist and novelist Jimmy Breslin, worked for Cocoa Today as a copyboy, the newsroom term for a "go-fer."

Cocoa Beach was known for being the hot East Coast surfing spot. With his passion for surfing, young Jimmy consented to community college only in Cocoa.

Name recognition won him the part-time newspaper job.

Having pitched coverage of the Apollo launch aboard the cruise ship to my editors, they consented if the cruise line would grant a pro bono.

In exchange for passage, I would submit stories nationally to Gannett newspapers.

One night two weeks before my flight to New York, I introduced myself to young Jimmy.

"Your dad's my favorite journalist," I told him.

"Any way we could meet?"

Young Jimmy called home.

Breslin was past deadline on his latest book, *Without End, Amen,* his wife said.

But since your plane arrives early Sunday morning, take a cab to the house for breakfast.

More excited about meeting Breslin than the trip itself, I was riding high as the cab pulled in front of the Tudor home in Queens.

Tripping over empty milk and Almaden wine bottles on the side porch, I was quickly greeted into the kitchen by Breslin's wife

Breslin himself was unshaven, seated at the kitchen table in a t-shirt and shabby long pants.

He was holding a steak in both hands, gnawing the last meat from the bone.

"So you're Jimmy's friend," he said, extending a greasy hand.

The table chairs were piled high with magazines.

Feeling at ease, I hopped up onto the kitchen counter.

"What can I get you? Coffee, juice, milk, eggs, beer…"

"Beer," I quickly countered.

"Rosemary," he said grinning,

"Get Jimmy's friend here a beer."

I knew the legend of Breslin and his penchant for bars and people who lived on the street. He wrote about New York's underground and late-night characters.

Having a Sunday-morning beer in our first stage of introduction served as a bond for the candid lifestyle he embraced.

"Where you staying in the city?" Rosemary asked. The ship wouldn't pull out until the next afternoon.

"I don't know," I honestly replied. "Never been to New York. A friend suggested I stay on 42nd Street."

Breslin was aghast. He believed the sun rose and set on New York. No one had not ever been there before, especially a writer. Rosemary's motherly instinct rose to the forefront.

42nd Street in 1972 was the hellhole of prostitutes and pickpockets. This was the nicer element. Now it has been cleaned up and Disneyfied.

"You can stay in Young Jimmy's room," she insisted.

Breslin apologized for having to work. "I'll have a couple of my girls who type my manuscripts take you on a city tour," he offered. "Then tonight we can go out drinking."

At 3 a.m., after making the rounds at his favorite haunts, we sat in the kitchen polishing off conversation with a hamburger. Breslin and Mailer had once run for city office, more as an inside joke than serious endeavor, and almost won. Another election was coming soon.

Like most enterprising journalists, I was thinking ahead to be shipboard with Mailer for a week. "How is the best way to meet him?" I asked, finishing off the last bite of the evening.

The next day, as I waited for the cab to arrive, Breslin handed me an envelope. "When you see Mailer, give him this from me," he said.

His message was flippant, intended obviously as an introduction. "Filing deadline is coming. Are you game?"

It was signed Jimmy.

SUPPLEMENT:

Why the Astros Don't Want Me Anymore

Original newspaper article written by Captain Madness Himself
Published in Florida Today newspaper April 1972

'Why the Astros Don't Want Me Anymore'

Or, 'You Can't Catch a Right-Handed Ball

With a Left-Handed Glove

By Edwin E. Riley Jr.

Sunrise writer Edwin E. Riley Jr. spent a week recently working out with the Houston Astros in their spring training camp in Cocoa. Needless to say, he didn't make the team, but he did get a good taste of what spring training is all about. Here is his account.

So you're going to be a George Plimpton?" he asked.

"Not exactly," I said. "Not crazy enough to swing on a trapeze. That's unhuman. Or play professional football. Ummmm. Brutal."

"But Plimpton played professional baseball, too, didn't he?"

I didn't really know, because I'm not really a Plimpton fan, never having read one of his books. But the message was coming across.

The guy just kept rambling on, talking about workman's compensation, family insurance, fractured skulls and after the half-hour oration, succinctly summed up his advice with, "why don't you enter a beer drinking contest instead?"

DAY BEFORE SPRING
TRAINING SUNDAY

Now if you'll just sign these forms," Tal Smith was saying, handing the papers in triplicate across his desk.

Smith is a cautious man. Rightly so. He's vice president and director of player personnel for the Houston Astros Baseball Club.

And here I was, over the hill at 29 as far as minor leaguers go, getting ready to go into spring training just as if I were competing for a position with the team.

I would get the same considerations. Furnished a uniform, assigned a locker . . . oh, yes, and first aid treatment.

The form put all the risk on me. Nice guys, the Astro management. But nice doesn't mean taking the responsibility for an inexperienced writer-turned-ballplayer for a week.

Not that I minded signing a release for liability. It was just the innuendo that shook me.

"What position do you plan on playing," Smith asked.

"After reading this," I said, "the one farthest from the batter."

Smith and I finished the formalities and went to the Astro dining room for introductions with the coaching staff.

"We're going to treat you as a player to make it as realistic as possible," said slender Bob Lillis, former shortstop and director of minor league instruction.

And then he asked the inevitable question about my previous baseball experience and just sighed and shook his head when he heard the answer.

So did Dale Ford, an umpire from Johnson City, Tennessee who runs the Houston dressing room when he's not on the field.

Dale issued my uniform and he chose green out of four stocking color choices.

"I guess the color is apprepo," I said, and returned fully suited for an appraisal from the staff.

"Well, do I look like a baseball player?" I asked, standing with my legs spread real wide, hands pressed against the back pockets, just like the big leaguers do it on television.

"A reasonable facsimile," someone said.

"One thing's wrong," said Cliff Early, pitching coach, a grin breaking out all over his face.

"To make you look like one of the regular players, you've got to cut your hair."

"You just gave me a good title for my story," I told him.

"What's that?"

"The shortest career of a minor league player."

MONDAY MORNING
(BRIGHT AND EARLY)

If you live in the dorms, the man comes around when the roosters start crowing, banging on the doors.

Time to hop out of the sack and eat breakfast.

One thing about athletes. They get fed good. Whoooooeeeee. Hotcakes, bacon, sausage, biscuits, juice, milk. As much as the stomach can hold.

For a reason.

Tal Smith summed it up in the meeting after breakfast.

"Whenever you have a baseball uniform on it's time for you to go to work.

"This is your profession. It's no longer a game."

Work is right.

Starting with the shin splint exercise.

"Forward."

"Back."

"Hollllldddd it."

"Push a little bit."

"Get your tail in."

The exercise stretches leg muscles so they won't tighten up later.

Then once around the ball park and calisthenics. Some aren't too bad. The old standard side-straddle-hop. Kids call them jumping jacks.

But there were others. They didn't call them by name, but I've got a name for them. Agonizers would be too nice. The editor blipped out what I wanted to say. "Wouldn't be proper language for a family magazine."

Next came the light warm-up. Pairing off. Tossing the ball.

This guy didn't know what it meant to throw slow and easy. Every pitch he burned in like the world pennant was at stake.

I couldn't have told him to slow it down if I wanted to. Like so many players today, he speaks Spanish . . . only.

So I winced quietly to myself and kept tossing them back.

Now I'm telling you all this so you'll know what it's like out there on the field.

In the broiling sun. All hot and sweaty.

Always doing something. Never stopping until it's time to go in.

Definitely not the old sandlot rest-when-you-feel-like-it game.

Continued

105

'Next came the warmups. Tossing the ball. This guy didn't know what it meant to throw slow and easy.'

TODAY'S SUNRISE

And when the light warmup was finished, the players hit the field, most positions standing three to four feet apart.

So to keep everyone busy while waiting for the batter to hit the ball, someone hits grounders to the second basemen. And someone right near him hits flies to the outfielders, and another bats to shortstop and third base.

All which means the balls are going in every which-a-direction like bees on a cola can at the same time keeping an eye on the batter so the ball won't get you while you aren't looking.

I picked up the first bat I saw and started popping grounders to second base.

"You need fungo."

"Huh?"

"Fungo," Latin coach Epy Guerrero repeated. Thought he might mean fungus.

Nawwwww. Ridiculous.

Why would I need fungus to hit a few balls. And what kind of fungus?

First day confusion.

Here I was, Monday morning after the big pep talk, something about separating the men from the boys, and this foreign coach was hollering something at me that sounded like the Spanish version of fungus.

This was after calistentics and the green and blue teams were altogether on this one field.

The infielders infielded. The outfielders bunched in little groups and outfielded. The pitcher pitched. The batter batted. And while all this was going on, someone stood along the bases and hit balls to the first baseman. Another popped them to the shortstops. The second basemen got the full treatment, too.

And the whole time someone was at bat and the coach had told me just before he started yelling "fungo" to hit to the second basemen.

Which I was doing. Right proud of myself too. Just knocking the ball right between the pitcher and third base . . . without hitting them.

Maybe, just maybe, I thought, baseball is a slow game because so much time is spent getting the fungus before practice and getting rid of it before bedtime.

"FUNGO!"

"Fungo bat," he said.

"Ohhhhh. Bat."

I understand bat, so I walked over to the bag full of bats, but not a single one had fungus on it.

And coach Epy, he stood there looking at me like I was some kind of nut or stupid or something and for the life of me I just couldn't figure out what he was talking about so I just fessed up, real quiet like, hoping no one else would hear.

"Psssssst," I said, leaning over to the coach. "What in the hell is fungo?"

No need to say anymore. You can imagine the rest and while you're imagining, laugh real hard . . for Ely.

A fungo, by the way, is a lightweight, extra long bat. Gives more leverage to the hitter.

"You keep hitting them balls one after another with a regular bat and pretty soon your arms will feel like they're going to drop plumb from the sockets," Ely explained.

LESSON NO. 1 — Fungo is not the fungus.

> **TUESDAY MORNING**
> **(WAY TOO EARLY)**

Playing baseball with professionals borders on insanity, my body decided Tuesday morning as it groaned in harmony with the alarm.

Truthfully, I am a pretty active person. I dig surfing, bicycling, frisbee. Anything bordering on play. For short intervals.

Now an all day affair is something else. And bound to take its toll. On the muscles.

A bit sore? Yes.

Second doubts about a second day?

Yes, yes!

But I went anyway.

And it was worse than I thought

Because on Tuesday, lovely sunshiny Tuesday, the regimen started right on the stroke of nine.

"Hands against the wall. Forward Back." Shin Splint exercises.

"All right. Let's go. Let's go!"

And you run your fanny around the field until you find the place everyone has stopped and join ranks.

Just like the military in many ways. Midnight curfew, even.

And the $30,000 prima donnas nonwithstanding Midnight. Or a fine.

And the exercises. And the lunchroom. Uniforms at lunch. No cleats. But not barefoot. Put on sandals or palm fronds or something. Just don't get your gritty toes on the lunchroom floor.

No uniforms at breakfast, though. Another rule.

Not that the rules are hard to take. No inferences, PLEASE. Just rules. The way it is. Like the military.

Early spring training.

Learning the fundamentals. Getting in shape. Forgetting bad habits, acquiring good ones.

And anywhere you go, any workout, you RUN. No idle time.

Different from a lot of clubs, the players say, that leave you standing around, maybe waiting on someone to tell you what to do, or just waiting for the ball to head in your direction.

Not so with the Astros, and the players appreciate it.

Remember. They're young. Fighting for a position on the team. Working through the ranks. Sitting around will get them nowhere. Eager. Anxious. And the coaching staff makes sure they're kept busy. Active nine to noon. Never sitting. Never resting. Taboo. It's what the kids need. What they'll get. It's the training they respect. And the kind of training that has made the Astros a big name in baseball.

Not that it's a particular delight of a 29-year-old writer who wouldn't object at all to just a short rest period.

But like coach Tony Pancheoco put it jokingly: "I'm gonna tell you this kid. I'm gonna give you some instruction, but if you can't cut it, you'll have to become a writer or something."

Tony's a funny guy. A great one, too. Has to be one of the greatest coaches around. Says everything simple. So simple, it sounds easy. Until you try it. And what's more surprising, a lot of the things he tells you that sound easy are as easy as he tells them. So he's got to be good.

He tells you how you can't hit the ball in the batting cage because your left shoulder is hiked up in the air like a cloud. So you drop your left shoulder like he tells you and raise your right and before you know it you're hitting instead of whiffing. Great change of pace.

So who's Tony Pancheoco? What right has he to tell anyone how to swing a bat and steal a base?

Tony has 28 years right. He's been around. Newport to Havana to Charleston to West Palm to Cocoa to Columbia and on over onto the second page in the organizational yearbook.

Regardless. Tony is Tony. More important. He

Continued

'Athletes eat well.'

'Second day . . . plenty sore.

With trainer Bob Cooper.

'Somehow the ball stuck in my glove. Mickie Mantle couldn't have done better.'

knows how to communicate. And he knows baseball. Great combination.

Now on any given day, the routine goes something like this.

Spend 25 minutes hitting and fielding ground balls. Then move on to hitting. Then bunting. Next ball tossing. Finally baserunning.

With no pause.

"Hey. Baseball players no sit down," one of the Latin coaches yelled in my direction.

No they don't. Not until lunch at noon. Three hours since exercise. Lunch break.

Hit the field. Gametime. A scrimmage for two squads. The royals and orange.

For the others, batting practice. Hitting, fielding, running. And conditioning. Eight flat-out 50 yarders. You say 50 yards doesn't sound like much, maybe.

Think of it another way. Four football fields. Makes me break out in a sweat just thinking.

Tired? Oooooo boy! And how. Which way is up? It's been a long day. Got a few stiff muscles, too. So I get home, take a shower, and watch zzzz, and watch zzzz, a little televisi,zzzzzz . . .

WEDNESDAY (WHERE'D THE NIGHT GO)

Ready to hit the old field?
Am I ready!
Just ask.

I'd rather have a dental appointment.
"It hurts," I said.
"Where?"

"Pick a place. Anyplace. Head to toe."

But I wasn't the only one. The other guys, the real professionals, they hurt too. Eased my pain a bit.

Jackie Brandt is a hardnose coach. Or he pretends to be. A real tuffy, Brandt describes himself. The essence of discipline. Strictly from the old school.

Doesn't like crybabies. No sir. Can't cut it. Get the hell out.

Brandt says he doesn't like the change. Orders from up high. Having to pamper, according to his definition, the kids coming into baseball today. Much rather knock some heads together, he'll tell you.

He talks of the days when the game was rough. Real rough. Back during his heyday in the National league with St. Louis, New York, San Francisco, and later the American league with Baltimore.

How he broke a catcher's leg one time sliding into his shin guards, cleat first, legs thrust back, then a good heavy blow. Getting even for a dirty move the catch put on one of his teammates the day before.

Cutthroat. Getting the next guy. "And we'd get him sooner or later," Brandt says. "Just let someone intentionally mess up one of ours, and he'd know it was coming . . . and expected it!"

This was back in the 50s and early 60s and times have changed and Jackie Brandt is trying to adjust and says it's not easy.

He lifted his cap. Crew cut. "Used to be everyone had one like this," he said. "No more."

Jackie Brandt plays tough. Says he likes the old way better. Would like to chew the players out like a drill sergeant.

Jackie Brandt is a phony.
He's more gentle than a puppy.
A great guy.
And in the same breath he's telling how great it

Coach Tony Panacheoco gives batting instruction.

would be to give the fuzzy-faced kid mortal hell, he says sometimes it's necessary to crawl on a kid sometime and he sees them take the criticism "until I hurt all inside."

Sure. Jackie Brandt is tough.
So are dandelions.

If you had a "nice guy machine", Jackie Brandt would be one of the first in the batch.

Now don't get me wrong. Pro baseball's no badminton match. Hardly!

Rough and tumble. Guys get hurt. All by themselves. Breaking legs sliding. Front teeth laying on the ground when a ball takes a bad hop. Concussions.

And like vice president Tal Smith said the first morning, "This is your profession. It's no longer a game."

Big money involved. Thirty, forty grand for some. The promising few. Still under 20. Not old enought to buy a beer. In the chips, some of these kids.

Makes for pressure. You bet.

Take catcher Harlan Keller. Born 1951, Keota, Oklahoma.

In his third year. Disabled two of the three. Shoulder operation.

Trying to come back now. But he's got the pressure where it hurts.

"I've got ulcers and everything," he says, knowing he can't sit on the bench and play ball at the same time.

He's looking to the day when he'll face 40,000 fans on the big field. So are all the others. This makes it tough. Competitive. "Dog eat dog," Harlan puts it.

THURSDAY (CAME MUCH EASIER NO ACHES, NO PAIN)

The final day.
Number 16 jersey.
A neophyte. Sunday to Thursday.

Now I know a little. No. A whole lot. About professional baseball, players, coaches.

What it takes.

The hours. Dedication. Agility.

And personally, I learned how to hit the ball. Like

the pros. Drop the left shoulder. Hike the right. Hold the bat high. Swing free and easy. Don't try to kill it. Meet it. Keep an eye on the ball. Start to finish.

Thursday. Four days later. The exercises came easier. Lunch could be swallowed. Routine took hold. Reflexes improved. The coaching was paying dividends. The ball didn't look like a rocket anymore. A missile, maybe. But slower than a rocket.

And on Thursday came the climax. The big game.

Standing at the plate. Facing the pitcher. Head of the lineup. Right field for the Astros. At the plate. Bat in hand.

I stood on the fringe of the batter's box, reached down, grabbed some red dirt, rubbed the palms together, wiped them on my pants legs and turned to the catcher.

"Isn't that the way they do it?" I said, grinning, and stepped to the plate.

Wind up. Here it comes. Low and outside. Ball one.

"Ahem," I said, stepping back. "Could you ask him to throw it underhanded?"

The catcher has a great sense of humor. He chuckled.

Next pitch, the bat connected, shortstop to first base. OUT!

Two outs later, I hit the field. Right field. Sure enough, couple batters later it came my way. High in the sky. Higher than an airplane. Way up there. Just drifting around. And me running around in circles trying to get under it. With so much at stake, too. These two guys on base. A flub, they would surely score.

Somehow the ball hit the glove and ———

All the coaches had turned out to watch me play.
So did the management.
They were all cheering.
Mickie Mantle couldn't have done better.

And the next inning, second time at the plate, on a 3-2 count (that's three balls two strikes) I let go on the next pitch and drove it good, clean and solid between first and second base for a single.

Could have been 100,000 in the stadium and I wouldn't have felt better. All these guys yelling what a goody I had done.

The next batter drove one in perfect position for a double play and the second baseman, last year's number one draft choice, was at the right place at the right time and right smack dab in the baseline.

And here I was, running full steam ahead, thinking all the time I had the right-of-way. Think again. I didn't. He did. And I hit him head on, last year's number one draft choice, just like a brick wall, pulling a neck muscle and scraping a knee in fine fashion in the process. And all the while the guys on the bench, knowing full well I had pulled a boo boo, cheered, "Way to go, Ed. Kept him from making a double play."

Well. That's the way it went. One week with professional baseball.

And after the game, the players and the coaches came around and we shook hands. And Tal Smith, the head honcho, said "come to my office after you get showered and we'll talk about a contract."

The Houston Astros. Greatest group of guys, coaches and players, you'd ever want to find anywhere.

Makes you want to be one of them.
. . . "say Tal. About that contract . . ." ●

109

SUPPLEMENT:

Clown for a Day

Original newspaper article as written
by Captain Madness on an undercover assignment
Published in Florida Today newspaper April 1972

CLOWN for a Day...

By
Edwin E.
Riley Jr.

Nervous funnyman Edwin Riley anxiously awaits the clown call.

Painting on the patsen face is easy; it's making the kids laugh that is tough.

Sunfunny time in the ring as the clowns 'make the audience happy.'

Photo by Al Satterwhite

Continued

113

Clown for a Day

Continued

me to shut one eye and not talking too much about August clowns.

"These August clowns," I continued, "you know, the kind I am. What did you say they do?"

"OK. Now close your eyes just a little," Levoie said, dabbing here and there and everywhere.

"Uh, Levoie," I said. "Now about this August clown."

"Oh, yeah, the August clown," he said.. "He can take the falls."

"The falls?" I winced.

"You know, slapstick and stuff like that."

The subject was better left alone. After all, a clown shouldn't panic in the face of duty.

A hat topped off the outfit.

"Time to go," Levoie announced. "The clown walk."

It was the start of the circus. Clowns go first, parading around the arena.

Several of the clowns gathered around, the bills of their caps poking me in the eyes, inspecting my face close up.

"Nice job," someone said.

"Un-hum," the midget nodded. "Nice job." Waiting for the music to crank up, Levoie talked about how "it's hard to believe a clown drinks or cusses."

They just don't. Like Santa Claus, clowns can do no wrong. "An escape for the younger generation and the older," Levoie said, as I stumbled around in shoes the size of tennis rackets.

"Excuse me," I whispered, trampling over one of the other clowns' feet.

Levoie's sense of duty was undaunted. "When you're out there, you'll sense someone is watching you, because there is someone watching you somewhere and this is something you must always remember."

Clowns have long hair, big noses, and extra large shoes. Clowns just do, and the nose goes on last, held fast with surgical adhesive. A big red bulb with tiny slits for breathing.

"Get my nose custom made with holes to fit the nostrils," said one of the clowns who has been around for some time. "I'm a nose breather," he said, "and those tiny slits just don't get it."

Levoie was waiting on the band to start the introductory music for the clowns and he talked more about the circus as an escape.

Like the time in Texas when a tornado almost tore the whole town down. Financial losses that would take a lifetime for many to recoup. Not to mention the folks who were laid up in the hospital, nursing physical wounds, and the funerals. And while all this was going on, the pandemonium, the grief, they went to the circus, Levoie said.

Levoie started out on the trapeze, but he was up there on a swing, high above the people, swinging back and forth.

He wanted more personal contact, a chance to see a kid or an adult smile back, and clowns go out into the arena 14 times a show. Which gives Levoie 14 chances to reach out and touch someone.

"Each performance is a new audience," he was saying, getting as serious as a clown can get. "I've got to win them over, make them happy. If I can do something to make them happy, that's the essence of it."

DA- DA- DE- DA-DEE- DAHHHHHHHHH. Every clown's stomach turns into butterflies when the trumpet sounds the signal. Tomfoolery time. Once around the ring.

"C'mon," Levoie said. "Just stick close."

I couldn't move. "C'mon," Levoie said again. "My foot's caught."

The big shoe was trapped under some servicewires and Levoie reached down, pulled up the cables, then took off around the ring, practically in a run, trying to catch up with the rest of the troupe.

A clown's life is not so easy, I was thinking trying to put one foot in front of the other instead of on top of another.

Halfway around the ring Levoie and I ganged up on a family five rows up. Mom, Dad, and the two kids.

"Ying, ying, ying, woooooooooo," I said. Clown talk, I decided, for lack of anything else to say. The kid was a real smart aleck. "You're a stupid clown," said the five-year-old.

"Stupid, who me?" I countered, poking myself in the chest,and giving a shrug of the shoulders. "Yeah, you can't talk right."

Levoie was in hysterics. "Dumb kid," I mumbled as we went back ringside.

Right out front. The place you dream about as a kid.

How much fun it would be. How you get there, being a clown. Whomping each other over the head. So much fun.

Dancing around. Big bright lights everywhere. And the elephants . . . watch where you step.

Back in the wings again clown Don Marshburn was talking about how you have to be " a little crazy" to be a clown.

He was trying to line up an interview with Levoie from his home in chilly Des Moines and couldn't get through to him. The circus was playing in Salt Lake City 1,000 miles away so Don made the trip, hoping for the best.

"You must be crazy," Levoie told him "coming this far."

Don agreed and got the job.

Ray Lesperance is a clown and he put on a *Continued*

'Un-hum,' the midget nodded, 'nice job.'

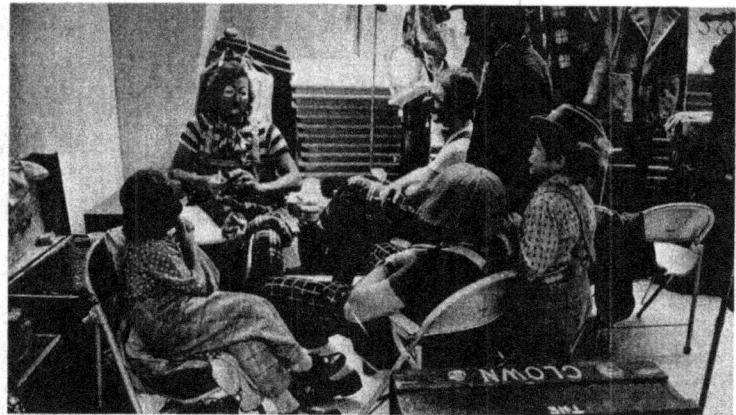

The clowns gather around to recount the experience after 'The Greatest Show on Earth.'

Clown for a Day

Continued

chicken suit, a fuzzy yellow thing with a big red beak.

"You're going to lead me around this time," he said. "Just walk ahead, I'll stall, and you try to make me move ahead. Got it?"

"Sure."

Ray's been with the circus two years now, coming from a Boston band called Gino Kenny and the Conservatives. Al Jolson type music, he described it.

Used to do some imitations back then. Tiny Tim, Mrs. Miller. "Did all right playing the drums," Ray said, pulling the chicken head over his own, but he read an article about being a clown, found it too tempting to pass up, and now he's a clown in a chicken outfit. "Wouldn't change it for the world," he said.

The cue came and off we went. "Hey, look at the chicken, look at the chicken," the little girl screamed, and Ray the ex-drummer was hamming it up for the kid as I trailed ahead.

I turned back, walked up to Ray, motioning to come on. He nodded no, the beak swaying back and forth.

So I stomped on his chicken foot.

"Ouch," he said. "That hurt, dammit."

The kids were howling, watching Ray the Chicken hopping up and down on one leg, nursing a sore foot.

What an opportunity to release frustrations, I decided, hitting the chicken in the head with my hat when he balked the next time.

"You sure do get carried away with this stuff," he grumbled.

"Yeah, but the kids love it. Listen to them laugh."

"Probably my mother out there," Ray quipped.

Back in the dressing room Ray rubbed his foot

and warned the other clowns to "beware of the 'Stomper,'" the new clown with big feet.

Levoie was passing out musical instruments for the band session. Everyone plays something. I got a kazoo.

A kazoo looks like a shrunken flute with holes in both ends.

Just hum into it, and it makes the same kind of shrill noise like a comb and tissue paper.

I was the last one out and at center ring, just before exiting, the main spotlight was on me, the big footed clown with a kazoo.

"Get to it," Levoie whispered. "You're in the clown spotlight. It's an honor few get."

And that's all it took, being a natural born ham. I jumped and skipped and hopped and blew the kazoo like crazy and Levoie was getting frantic 'cause I wouldn't leave the ring. All the other clowns had gone off stage, and I just jumped around until Levoie grabbed my arm and pulled me out of the spotlight."

"That was fun," I said, giving Levoie the biggest clown grin of the whole evening.

"Jesus," he said, shaking his head. "I thought you'd never leave."

"'Yeah, but didn't you hear the kids laughing?"

"Sure, but ... good grief, Ed. You want to get them laughin so hard it'll give them a stomach ache?"

Levoie's a good sport, I decided.

The big finale was the clown car. Seventeen clowns jammed inside a compact car, windows rolled up.

"You get in next to last," someone said. They piled in one at a time. Scrunching up, laying down, taking up every available inch."

"Now it's your turn. Just turn around backwards and wedge yourself on them."

I went to climb in, groping over the bodies stacked dashboard high.

"Eiiiiii," someone shrieked. "Not that way."

A big chorus of jeers went up as I climbed back out.

"Try it again," said the last clown to climb in.

"Okay. Here goes."

Too bad all this took place outside the auditorium. The crowd would have loved the moans.

"You've got the sharpest elbows in the world," someone on the bottom said.

Trouble with the feet again. They wouldn't fit.

"Lift them higher," said the outside man. "I'll squeeze them in up against the windshield."

The last guy squeezed in and the door was closed. It was no place for anyone with a touch of claustrophobia.

The car went round and round inside the auditorium, in and out of the rings, finally stopping center stage, and one by one we climbed out.

The crowed was delirious with laughter. Three of the clowns started swatting me with anything handy. Probably the ones I sat on in the car.

Then it was all over, and back in the dressing room Levoie and the others were standing around as I pulled off the big bulb nose and dropped the suspenders.

"You know, you don't make a half bad clown," Levoie said, and the others joined in, saying how I made a good clown, everybody except for Ray the Chicken who was sitting in the corner rubbing his foot.

Makeup comes off easily. Just a little soap and water.

But the smile was still on my face as I felt the Greatest Show on Earth and went back to work for a living. ●

Edwin E. Riley Jr. is a TODAY staff writer.

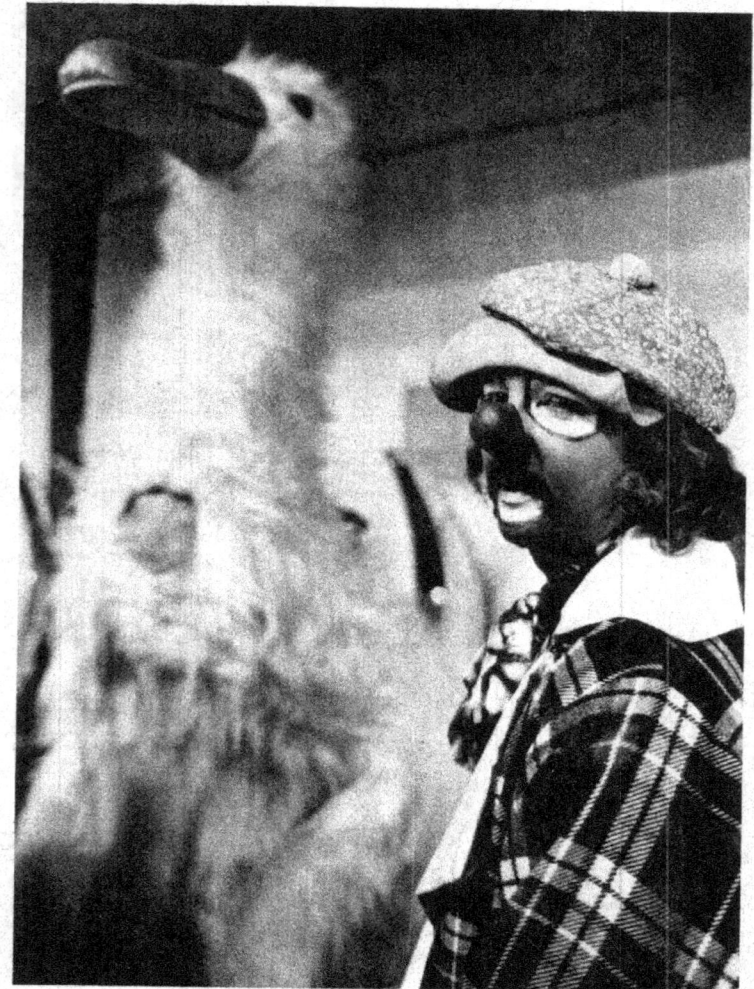

'Ray the Chicken' and 'Stomper Riley' after their bout in center ring.

Collective "clown" consciousness.

Dressed and ready to go on, Riley listens for tips from his fellow clowns.

118

*L–R: Norman Mailer's wife Carol Stevens, Norman Mailer, me,
an unknown travel agent, and New York Times writer Tom Buckley
dining aboard the SS Statendam.*

ON BOARD THE STATENDAM

*"Some moments are so human,
only a rocket launch can compete."
— from the Captain's Log*

My cab driver was the brother of "Marvin the Torch," an arsonist and one of Breslin's column characters. Breslin always summoned him to deliver houseguests. He had a certain New York rough-edged panache guaranteed to entertain.

At my request, we stopped en route to the docks for a case of beer that I hoisted over one shoulder as I walked up the gangplank. A little stash, I figured, for my cabin locker.

Mailer had yet to arrive. "I'll let you know when I see him," said the amicable PR hack. "Why don't you go sign up for a dinner table."

A steward in all whites sat behind the double glass doors with his passenger list.

"Go ahead and put Norman Mailer at my table," I told him. "We're together."

He was skeptical. Said it was not standard procedure. I insisted, staring him into submission. Relenting, he gave me two extra passes, one for Mailer and another for his fifth wife, Carol Stevens.

Back in the lobby, I was signaled by the PR hack, pointing to Mailer who had just arrived.

"Norman Mailer?" I asked, and introduced myself, explaining that I had stayed with Breslin as a weekend house-guest. "I have a letter for you," I said, "so I took the liberty to assign us the same dinner table so I could get it to you," handing him the chits.

"I didn't know what to think," Mailer confessed as we finished dinner. "I told Carol, 'this guy's got balls', but what are we going to do if we can't stand being with him?" The table assignment was for the entire week.

We hit it off. Tom Buckley, a writer for The New York Times, television commentator Hugh Downs, Carol, Mailer and myself became a team. Always inquiring, a journalistic trait, we picked scientists' brains looking for openings. You never know when something might fall out.

On launch night, we all sat around the lounge with other writers, waiting for lift-off. As common with most space shots, the countdown gets postponed at least once. Conversation focused on Isaac Asimov, the world's most prolific science fiction writer and recluse. Obviously nervous, he was guzzling drinks like the world was soon ending.

"Why are you here if this makes you so miserable?" I ventured.

"Feel I owe it to my readers," he explained. "This is the final manned Apollo mission."

Asimov hated travel. Even to his neighborhood grocery. Confinement on a cruise ship for a week to him was excruciating.

Hugh Downes was edgy too. Cabin fever. Even Mailer was anxious to walk on land. I had tried earlier for permission to go ashore for the afternoon. The ship, however, was in a restricted area. Concessions had been made for us to be there. The answer was a definitive "no."

Downs volunteered to do a play by play over the ship's intercom, take his mind off his discomfort. A storm system lay to our south. NASA was monitoring it closely. God forbid we get a 24-hour delay. Everyone in our close quarters would freak out.

Just before midnight, we got the word. Countdown had resumed. Asimov and I leaped from our chairs and headed for a prime spot along the ship's rail facing west toward Cape Canaveral.

As a writer, I had witnessed most Apollo launches, usually from the press site seen on TVs around the world for its famous countdown clock. This was a new perspective. The rocket would be coming towards us.

To a casual observer, the old Saturn rockets on ignition were far more spectacular and suspenseful than those post Apollo. Like suspended animation, they would hang as fire flared, and smoke billowed beneath.

No one can capture in words the sensory experience. Like looking directly into blaring sunlight, your eyes are telling you to close them. The thundering reverberation becomes deafening and fills your body in a haunting, yet exhilarating cadence.

Liftoff! Ooooohhhhsss and Ahhhhhhhhhsss. Some one-word exclamations came from those watching. Mostly sounds bordering on primal celebration.

Until the huge fiery ball took aim, it seemed, directly at the ship. Pleasure noises turned sour. In our down range path, Apollo 17 looked like a meteor gone mad. Awesome as the moment, there was pause for consternation.

At the brink of panic, the massive fireball lifted, and once more exultation replaced guttural sounds of trepidation.

I turned to Isaac. "Well, this being your first launch, what did you think?"

"Edwin, to quote the eloquence of all those around me, 'OH SHIT!'"

Here I was, standing next to one of the biggest names in world literature, and my quote was censored for general newspaper audiences.

"What the hell," I thought. "That's what he said, that's what I'm sending in over the wires."

Besides, 'OH SHIT' truly summarized what we all felt.

---

* The Holland America Line ship SS Statendam carried a group of notable passengers to watch the launch of the final Apollo 17 mission in December 1972.

Hosting a special reading of my newest book,
Go Naked To The Market, to a captive audience
on board the SS Statendam.

Me, Norman Mailer, and Tom Buckley
having lunch at Bluebeard's Beach Club
in the US Virgin Islands.

UNPUBLISHED AND EXCLUSIVE
Conversation With Norman Mailer

"All I can say, Norman, is this has been a hell of a lot of fun...
and just relish the peace."
— from the Captain's Log

Years later I was on the committee for the Miami International Book Fair held every November down in Miami. It's a week-long event, and in 1988 Norman Mailer was one of the key speakers.

He had free time to come over to my sailboat where we spent the afternoon sharing.

I had written down some questions in my mind that I would ask Norman should the occasion arise. The occasion did arise one blissful sunny afternoon and we found ourselves languishing in the cockpit of my sailboat, *Raconteur,* a 44-foot cutter-rigged CSY.

Norman turned out to be, in these later years, a generous gentleman in all respects despite his notorious reputation that mostly stemmed from his youthful days of fighting, boozing and womanizing.

When I explained that I had written down some questions to ask him, he agreed and said, "But first I want to know, How do you ever get any writing done living on a sailboat?"

"Unfortunately, usually I Don't," I said. "It's so peaceful and meditative. Puts you in a malaise. Writing gets pushed to the side burner. It's hard to get the juices flowing when you're so content."

The art of writing is fueled by a sense of urgency to share your thoughts with others. When you're sitting in the cockpit of a sailboat, you're in a dreamy womb. The essential womb of calmness and serenity. So, you can lose the drive to create.

"Now I have some questions for you," I said.

Sitting in the cockpit of the boat, we were so relaxed it was the perfect moment to ask the questions I had been pondering.

"First, Norman, what is the literary situation in America now?" I asked.

"I think my attitude will come out as I answer the questions," he responded.

"If you were giving advice to a young writer on the brink of fame, what would you say?" I asked.

"Try to keep the rebel artist in you alive no matter how attractive or exhausting the temptations," he answered.

"Why do you write?"

"I suppose I write because I want to reach people and by reaching them influence the history of my time a little bit," he said.

"How do you feel about sex?"

"How I feel about it personally is none of your business.

How I feel about it as a literary subject is something else. I believe it is perhaps the last remaining frontier of the novel which has not been exhausted by the nineteenth and early twentieth century novelists," he responded.

"Do you think the current censorship wave will make us a nation of mental eunuchs?"

"The situation is exceptionally complicated. There is not only a wave of censorship but there are counter waves which are opposed to censorship. I feel more optimistic about the general situation than I have in years. But this may conceivably be no more than a reflection in my present mood," he replied.

"Do you write to eat or eat to write?"

"Anyone who asks a question like that knows nothing about writers. Every serious novelist in the world obviously does both.

If he ate only to write he would be merely a dilettante or deadly small critic who is kept in a cage until his editor lets him out to devour a new book," Mailer said.

"Do you write before or after sexual activity, or during the periods you deny yourself such activity?"

"I've thought about this a lot, but I don't know that I have any definite feeling about the answer," said Mailer.

"What is your opinion of the current crop of artistic aspirants in Miami?

"I have a sincere feeling – perhaps it is no more than a hunch – that more than a few really exciting novels are going to come to from there in the next ten years. Provided, of course, we do not dip back into the Cold War again.

A Cold War is obviously equal to greater censorship, greater censorship is equal to greater fear, especially in serious writers, more anxiety and hence poorer work generally," he responded.

"Do you believe that there are good writers unable to find publication in America today?"

"If good writers write novels which are conventionally obscene or exceptionally radical, you can be sure that they would have one hell of a time getting their books published.

However, there are some good people scattered through the publishing houses and considering that no two publishing houses are even remotely the same, there is always a kind of chance to get a good but difficult book in bound covers," he said.

"Changing the topic, I have a more frivolous question. The question is, do you have political ambitions?"

"You can't grow up in America without thinking once in a while of becoming President. But since I'm an anarchist, I try not to think about that too much," he laughed.

"Are you a Freudian?"

"I believe Freud was a genius—an incredible, mighty discoverer of secrets, mysteries, and new questions. But the answers he gave were doctrinaire, death-like, and philosophically most dreary. Of the world's geniuses, he strikes me as being unique.

He had so little optimism, and it is rare to find a genius who does not love even angry optimism. Or, at the very worst, an apocalyptic view of the final disaster," he said.

"What quality do you most prefer in a woman?"

"Love infused with rich sensuality," he shared.

"What can ruin a first-rate writer?"

"Booze, pot, too much sex, too much failure in one's private life, too much attrition, too much recognition, too little recognition, frustration. Nearly everything in the scheme of things works to dull a first-rate talent.

But the worst probably is cowardice. As one gets older, one becomes aware of one's cowardice. The desire to be bold which once was a joy gets heavy with caution and duty.

And finally, there is apathy. About the time it doesn't seem too important anymore to be a great writer, you know

130

you've slipped far enough to be doing your work now on the comeback trail," he said.

"Norman, I have one last question. What do you think of the women's movement now?"

"I don't think that women have done much in developing their ideas. Can you tell me some new ones that have come out of Women's Liberation in the last decade or so?

What are they saying now they weren't saying fifteen years ago? What astonishing new thesis has *Ms.* Magazine come up with lately?

Many people respond supinely to totalitarian force. The women's movement at its worst is totalitarian – unforgiving, unfair, incapable of quoting accurately and quick to distort the deeds of its adversaries," he proclaimed.

"All I can say, Norman, is this has been a hell of a lot of fun," I said, "and just relish the peace," as we sat there watching seagulls gliding in the thermals overhead, the soft sounds of water gently caressing *Raconteur*'s hull.

I never tried to have this conversation published as an interview even though I had permission. At the time, my curiosity was sated, and I considered our time and talks sacrosanct. I guess timing is everything.

Same went for the afternoon we spent having lunch with Tom Buckley down at the beach in the US Virgin Islands.

We were staying at the resort called Bluebeard's Castle, in a hotel perched above the sea. From there, we took a shuttle down to their private beach club and restaurant. We swam out to a floating dock, where we lounged in the Caribbean sun and swapped stories.

We knew without saying that our private conversations then would remain unspoken and languish in this realm we call friendship.

Some authorities just can't take a joke.
I might just hijack your beer, but that's it.

HIJACKING AND SUGAR BEAR

"Some landings are smoother than others."
— from the Captain's Log

Two days later the S.S. Statendam pulled into port at St. Thomas, U.S. Virgin Islands. Mailer, his wife Carol, Buckley, Downs and myself got adjoining rooms at Bluebeard's Castle. We would all fly to our respective homes in two days. Meanwhile, we swam and drank and generally enjoyed being back on terra firma.

It was a heady experience.

When my plane landed at Miami International for a layover before my flight to Orlando, my adrenaline was pumping way off the charts.

What a week! Being a gregarious person anyway, I hit the bar in overdrive, sharing Apollo tales with strangers, in enthusiastic hyper gear, shoulder-length hair and all.

Didn't really compute in December 1972, that a rash of hijackings to Cuba had plagued Miami International. When I finally sat down at the boarding gate, I was greeted by a badge-flashing man in a dark suit and brown cordovans.

"Joe Mitchell, U.S. Deputy Marshall," he said, flipping the badge quickly and returning it to his coat pocket.

"Let me see some identification."

As I said, I was flying high, his request at the time seemingly benign. I pulled out my wallet and handed him a card. On it was a smiling picture of Sugar Bear. Big wide ears and a grin. My signature was on the bottom. It had come from my daughter's Sugar Pops cereal box.

Joe Mitchell didn't laugh. He just stepped back a pace, whipped out his radio, and called for backup.

Within seconds I was surrounded with brown suits and cordovans. No one seemed to appreciate the joke. I sensed from the guns and handcuffs that maybe it was a good time to cooperate.

"Could I see that badge again?" I asked, *sotto voce*. "Been a long week," I explained, quickly producing press credentials, passport, ship stubs, driver's license and every other legal document in my possession.

Seems I had been profiled due to enthusiasm and flowing hair as a potential hijacker. Mitchell wouldn't say who fingered me. A space buff, he was more interested in my escapade, dismissing his backup and sitting next to me.

We chatted amicably until my departure and exchanged personal address cards. "You ever get back to Miami," he said, "look me up. Enjoyed talking to you. And stay away from Cuba."

I did make it to Havana eight years later, taking my daughter for her 18th birthday. Few Americans even knew entry was being permitted. I was teaching at Miami-Dade Community College. One of my students, a travel agent, informed me.

We took a flight on Air Florida, toured Havana, drank daiquiris as Hemingway's old haunt, La Floridita, and dined at the famous Tropicana.

I never bothered to call Joe Mitchell and tell him how much fun we had.

Taking a breather in between bomb warnings at the snack bar.

FREELANCE STARVING

*"Sometimes the story **is** the job."*
— from the Captain's Log

"The only way to write is to write," Mailer had said during a talkfest as we lay on the floating raft in St. Thomas. I took his words to heart.

"So how was your week with all the writers and scientists?" asked the editor.

"Great!" I said. "I quit."

Mailer's idea about writing had a romantic ring. The downside is lack of income during the writing process. That's why writers are generally referred to as "struggling artists." In fact, most artists are usually referred to as "struggling."

With a wife and two kids and a rabbit left over from Easter (it seemed like a good idea at the time), I turned to free-lance writing to pay the bills. When I ran out of story ideas, I would hang out with Lucy who managed Cape Canaveral pier.

Once I wrote a story about her dog that had become a pier mascot. "Waldo" mostly got in the way. His favorite spot was where everyone coming and going had to step over Waldo. Like a big brown bear rug, he just lay there, even when someone accidentally would step on him.

Ocean piers are like magnets for characters. Many are sordid, like Walter, the crazier than a loon neo-Nazi storm trooper. Others, like Ben Logan, the senior surfer and former Tarzan, are just plain fun and interesting.

The pier was a great place to fall back on for story ideas. If for no other reason, the view was great.

And Lucy was good to bounce potential stories off. She managed the pier and ran the snack bar. Someone else the bar; another bait and tackle.

I hit a dry spell... several days and no story ideas. I was getting panicky. Freelancing is this way. If no stories are being circulated, no cash is coming your way.

Then Lucy told me she would be going out of town for the weekend. Her eldest daughter, who usually took over in her absence, was sick.

"I'll run the snack bar for you," I volunteered.

She looked at me dubiously. "Are you sure you want to?"

"Yeah, yeah, yeah," I interjected. Writers can be dangerous critters. They see stories in between the lines. I could pick up a few bucks and turn the experience into an article, I reasoned, tossing my idea back to Lucy.

"It gets frantic on weekends," she said. Lucy was justifiably hesitant. She knows human nature and can spot "laid back" like an eagle.

What's the big deal, I thought. A hot dog rotisserie, coffee maker, cola dispenser, hamburger grill, corn dog hot fryer, and pre-packaged snacks. "Let me think about it," she said.

Later I found out she had called everyone who had ever worked for her to no avail.

Out of sheer desperation, I got the gig.

Saturday morning started out slow. Here a coffee, there a cola. A couple of customers would amble in, maybe order fries and coke, then wander back down the pier to the beach.

The weather was postcard perfect, a precursor for a busy day. The first onslaught came earlier than I had imagined.

When one person orders for eight friends left basting in the sand, it doesn't take long for momentum to gather. Soon the counter stools are filled. People are generally impatient, I was learning.

"Isn't it ready yet? How much longer?

Can't you hurry? We're starving!"

No one seemed to notice it was only I working the entire concession. By noon, they were three deep in lines, and growing hostile.

"I'd like twelve dogs, four with chili (one of those without mustard), three with onions and ketchup, two with mayonnaise, and three plain. And give me six Cokes, two Pepsis, a Dr Pepper, an orange drink, grape soda, lemonade, and a glass of water while I'm waiting."

"No, instead make that three with chili, four with onions and ketchup, four orders of fries, a bag of chips, and do you have any cookies?"

I went over the edge. This was insane.

Five bucks an hour for this? I'd rather be back in the layaway department at J.C. Penny. At least people didn't glare at you with ravenous spitefulness.

I reached around the partition to the wall phone as if it were ringing.

In the bedlam of orders being given, no one would notice.

"YES," I answered loudly and dramatically.

"Yes sir. At once."

Still holding the receiver in one hand, I forcefully announced to the hungry throng that we had received a bomb threat.

"Everyone must clear the pier immediately," I declared.

Placing the receiver back to my ear, I continued my one-way conversation. "Yes, we're clearing the snack bar now," I said, shooing everyone towards the exit with my free hand.

In just a few minutes, you could hear the proverbial pin drop. All was quiet. I walked across to the bar and got a beer.

Back at my station, someone ambled up to the counter and ordered a burger. "No problem," I said.

A few more customers placed their orders. The rotisserie was cranking again. The fries were humming. During the lull, I had restocked. Everything was running smoothly.

For a while. And then we hit peak lunchtime. Pandemonium! Now they were standing four deep, shouting orders, waving pieces of paper with their requests. Every machine in the joint was in high gear.

I reached for the phone.

"Everyone out," I ordered. "Bomb scare."

Lucy was back at her post on Monday morning when I got there. "How did things go?" she asked.

"Smoothly," I said.

"Understand we had a few bomb scares," she said, staring deep into my eyes, looking for answers she already knew. "Like 10," she added.

"Yeah," I commiserated. "A weird weekend. Fortunately, no one got hurt."

"Except my sales. We were off 50 per cent."

"Look," I suggested, "you don't have to pay me for my time."

She didn't.

LIVING THE LIFE OF RILEY

A Scrapbook Collection
From the Womb
Fast Forwarding Through Life
Time Passes Like Dust in the Wind

"Memories aren't just what happened.
They're how we stitch the soul back together."
— from the Captain's Log

A boy and his watermelon slice.

Forever an avid reader.

Getting Your Child
Ready for School

Department of Health Flyer.

*Prepping for the cell phone future
(age 2.5).*

Early Swag.

Covering the Grand Opening Day of
Disney World for Florida Today.

Orlando Airport with
Florida Governor Claude Kirk on the left,
me in the center suited up,
on the way to a speaking engagement.

Covering an Apollo launch from the press site
(Spacecraft visible in the background).
L-R: Me on crutches from a basketball injury, unidentified person,
friend and reporter Frank Beacham.

Footnote: *Frank Beacham later collaborated with Orson Welles*
and helped produce The Cradle Will Rock,
a film inspired by real-life events surrounding Welles.

Last stand in the corporate world,
leaving behind suit and tie.
The tie, a metaphorical noose,
separates the head from the heart at the throat chakra.

"YOU...yes YOU! I dare YOU to be Yourself!!!"

Sailing away from regimented workplace rules and
regulations, and into a realm of serious writing...
aka freelance starving.

Hauled out for boat maintenance.

I stumbled upon a smuggling venture
that didn't quite make it, Bahamas.

*Escorting Ted Knight clothes shopping at Burdines
in Miami Beach before an appearance.*

"Ok students, take your seats. We're going to do
something different in this classroom—
learn how to think for yourself."
At Miami-Dade Community College.

Random pictures traveling life's highway

with Tai Chi and QiGong Master Huang Wei Lun
in Jackson Hole, Wyoming.

with Deva Premal and Miten at a yoga intensive in Miami.

Chatting with Deepak Chopra
at Shivananda Yoga Ashram
in Nassau, Bahamas.

with Snatam Kaur
and Sopurkh Singh.

With Menas Kafatos.

With Arn Gandhi, Mahatma Gandhi's grandson.

Captain Madness and his trusty companion, Dharma.

PAPER TRAIL

Letters, Clippings, and Correspondence
Collected Along the Way

"What remains is not what we said,
but what someone took the time to write down."
—from the Captain's Log

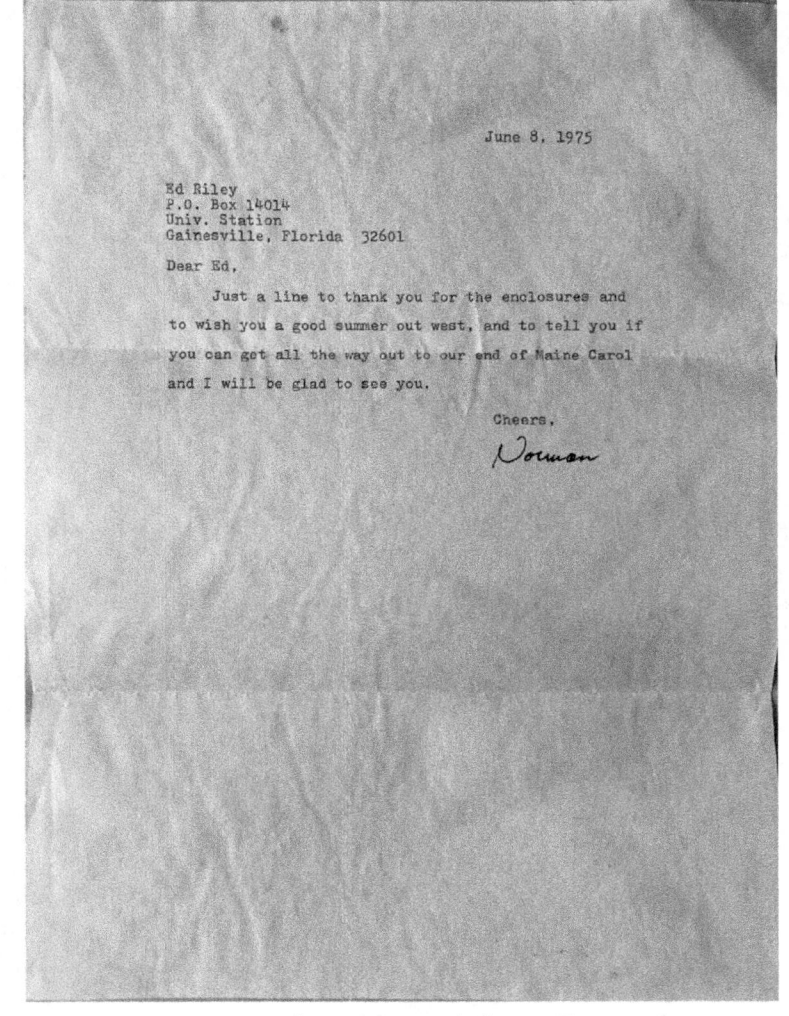

June 8, 1975

Ed Riley
P.O. Box 14014
Univ. Station
Gainesville, Florida 32601

Dear Ed,

Just a line to thank you for the enclosures and
to wish you a good summer out west, and to tell you if
you can get all the way out to our end of Maine Carol
and I will be glad to see you.

Cheers,

Norman

Letter from Norman Mailer, 1975.

February 25, 1977

To recommend Edwin E. Riley, Jr. for college teaching:

Met Riley April '75 at Energy and Consciousness conference,
University of Florida, with conferees Gary Snyder, Michael
McClure, Howard Odum and Henry Gomberg, we talked frequently
during three day weekend, he was helpful arranger and moderator.

We met again at Naropa Institute in Boulder, Colorado,
summer 1975, where he sat, meditated and participated in Jack
Kerouac School of Poetics .

Riley's interest in environmental energy proposals - as at
the Florida conference -- and Buddhist style willingness to
teach both discipline and openness puts him at one center of
modern poetic interests: i.e. interests of myself, Snyder,
McClure, Ferlinghetti in the ecological studies done via Odum
in Florida. I liked his participation at Naropa Institute
with myself, Philip Whalen, Gregory Corso, Anne Waldman,
William Burroughs, Robert Creeley, Peter Orlovsky and W. S.
Merwin. Riley one of the good English teachers in the nation
actually in field teaching and learning, as well as reading at
desk.

His interests argue sane intelligent Person; organizing
Energy Conference required patience, originality, and responsibility. Riley's writing suggests his willingness to face his
own mind. He is literate and articulate in front of large
crowds as participant at poetry readings.

So I hope you entrust him with the literary education of
your college students.

                              Sincerely,

                              Allen Ginsberg
                              Allen Ginsberg

*Letter of Recommendation from Allen Ginsberg, written
in support of my "Out Of The Box" teaching philosophy,
February 25, 1977.*

Professor launches literary magazine

Raconteur to aim for distinction

By DAN FROOMKIN
Herald Staff Writer

Edwin Riley is a storyteller and a name-dropper.

He will, for instance, talk a blue streak about how he became friends with Norman Mailer. Or about how he spent his first night in New York City at Jimmy Breslin's house.

But the story he's telling most often these days is about a man who creates a super-glossy literary arts magazine from scratch. It's a story he hopes will become true.

And the name he's dropping is Raconteur, which is what the magazine would be called.

Riley, a Miami Beach poet and part-time professor of creative writing and magazine production at Miami-Dade Community College, has grand plans for Raconteur.

Intended to serve as "a forum for writers and artists from the Palm Beaches to Key West," the three-yearly magazine would feature poetry, prose and artwork. At its heart, however — at least for the first issue, due in mid-September — would be nonfiction essays with a "cultural perspective," Riley said.

The time and place are ripe for such a magazine, he figures. Metamorphosis, the slick, fledgling Miami-Dade literary arts magazine for which Riley is faculty adviser, got a warm response after its first issue a year ago.

Further, Riley figures, the Miami area is no longer the "cultural wasteland" it was not long ago, and there are plenty of talented writers and artists around. In Key West alone, there are enough to keep a magazine afloat, he said.

Riley expects Raconteur to have a distinctly Southeast Florida style — innovative and tropical, laid-back but exciting. In short, sort of like Edwin Riley.

A man with straggly gray hair and a quick grin, Riley lives on a 44-foot sailboat, is partial to bare feet and fluorescent-pink shorts and runs the annual Bad Poetry Night at the Wet Point Cafe on Lincoln Road.

He has published two books of his own poetry — Go Naked to the Mirror and Confront Reality; You May Be a Salad — and won't tell his age. "Chronological, emotional or otherwise?" he asks. "We flip between several age groups here. "Say over 40."

A native of Columbia, S.C., where he acquired his drawl, Riley attended the University of South Carolina in two spurts — from 1960 to 1962, then 1967 to 1970. In between, he worked as a reporter for several newspapers in the Carolinas.

Afterward, he moved to Florida, worked in public relations, advertising and newspapers, got a master's degree in English at the University of Florida and embarked on a career of writing and teaching at community colleges.

Though he is already shinning up through "a fairly large number of submissions" and editing an article by environmentalist Marjory Stoneman Douglas for the debut edition, he is spending much of his time on another aspect of founding a magazine.

"I'm working my buns off trying to get funding together," he said. "It's going to take a pretty good amount of money to get it going."

To what he calls an effort to protect his editorial integrity, Riley is not accepting advertisements. So

RANDY BAZEMORE / Miami Herald Staff

Edwin Riley, aboard his 44-foot 'two-bedroom, two-bathroom condo afloat,' wants his magazine to be 'a forum for writers and artists from the Palm Beaches to Key West.'

Riley spends some of his time working on Raconteur in the magazine's temporary office on Lincoln Road, but he prefers working at a table on the deck of his sailboat, where he uses a conch shell as a paperweight.

He also embarked on boats. He's been living on them for 12 years. His latest — "a two-bedroom, two-bathroom condo afloat" is berthed at a tiny marina at the edge of Lincoln Terrace.

"This is a nice little enclave," he said, praising his view of downtown Miami at night and embarking on the tale of a recent visit to a nearby building by Don Johnson,

Melanie Griffith and Sophia Loren.

he has to raise the money from grants and contributions from individuals and corporations.

He expects the first year's budget to be a formidable $130,000.

After all, he plans a press run of 25,000 copies — half in English, half translated into Spanish — for each 52-page issue. He says he'll pay the market rate for material he publishes.

Riley has some supporters. Said literary activist Mitchell Kaplan, owner of Books & Books: "I think that there's always a need for a really good literary magazine here in Miami — and there's a market for it as well."

Riley himself is unhesitatingly optimistic. "Once that first issue comes out," he said, "there's not going to be any debate about the interest in it."

Sunday, Apr. 9 1989 ■ The MIAMI HERALD ■ 3

HOW TO BE PART OF RACONTEUR

Edwin Riley is accepting submissions for Raconteur, a new literary arts magazine set to debut in mid-September.

Raconteur will print poems, essays, articles and any kind of artwork that can be reproduced in a magazine.

Submissions can be sent to Raconteur Publications Inc., P.O. Box 811, Coconut Grove, Fla. 33233. For information, call 673-1302 or 532-1997.

Professor, poet, publisher.

Winner of the top national literary arts
magazine award among Universities
and Colleges in the United States.

MDCC literary arts magazine wins plaudits

By KAYLOIS HENRY
Herald Writer

When English composition teacher Edwin Riley decided to put together a literary magazine, he wanted something different.

He thinks he got it with Metromorphosis, a new literary arts publication for the Wolfson Center Campus of Miami-Dade Community College.

What makes this 26-page magazine different are the short stories and poems in English and Spanish as well as photographs of drawings, paintings and sculpture. Metromorphosis is a brightly colored, professional-looking magazine.

Riley said the magazine's publication in April also gives a measure of respect to the community college. There is a snobbery among the public that community colleges lack the quality of four-year institutions because of their transient student population, he said. The Wolfson Center's reputation is also hurt by its large number of international students, he said. But Riley saw these differences as a plus.

"I thought, 'What a gold mine!' We have such a diversity galore and a magazine could be an outlet for it, not a limitation," Riley said.

Metromorphosis was put together by students in a course taught by Riley. The magazine received a $10,000 budget from the administration to produce 10,000 copies.

Riley writes on the inside cover that Metromorphosis is the first literary magazine put out by the Wolfson Campus. But in 1975-76, the downtown campus produced Faces and Places, a literary paper that won numerous awards, said its former adviser Peter Townsend.

Reactions to the magazine have been good, students say. Layout and art director Mari "Pasita" Andino, said Metromorphosis helps show the community the talent of students who attend Miami-Dade.

"People who don't know me have called me to compliment it. I've gotten all good remarks, not a negative one yet," Andino said.

Vice President Eduardo Padron said the magazine is important because it serves as an outlet for students who otherwise would not have one.

"We spend money on the student newspaper and student art shows, it's time we spent some for writers," Padron said.

Metromorphosis is the only literary magazine published in the Miami-Dade Community College system. Eight years ago, the South Campus published a literary magazine called Southwind but stopped publishing because of budget cuts.

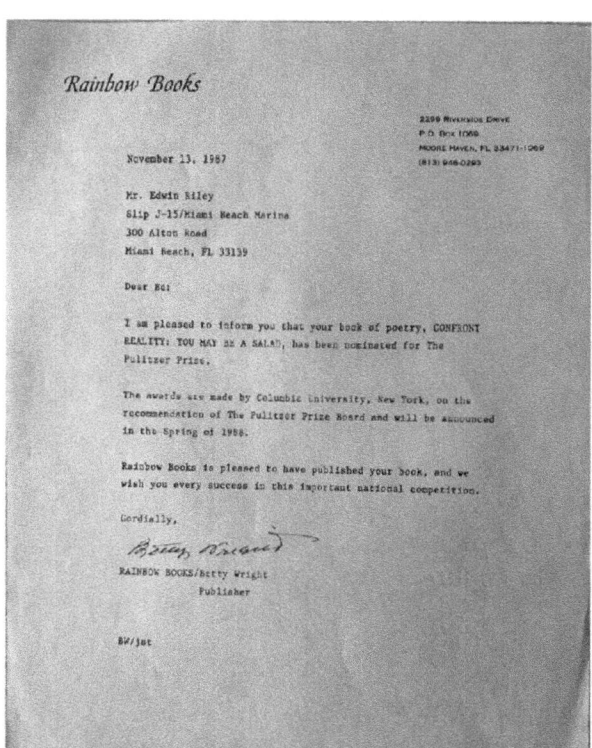

"*Your book of poetry... has been nominated for The Pulitzer Prize.*"
-Rainbow Books / Betty Wright.

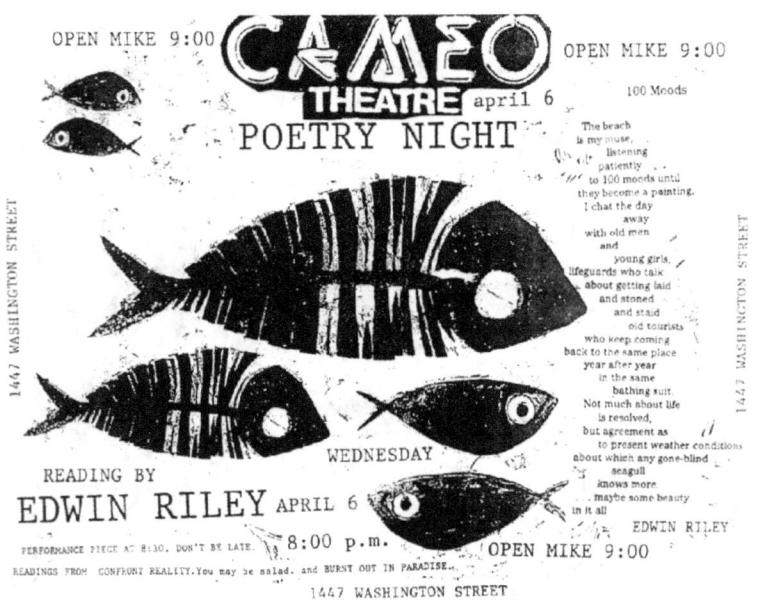

OPEN MIKE 9:00

CAMEO
THEATRE april 6

OPEN MIKE 9:00

100 Moods

POETRY NIGHT

1447 WASHINGTON STREET

The beach
is my muse,
listening
patiently
to 100 moods until
they become a painting.
I chat the day
away
with old men
and
young girls,
lifeguards who talk
about getting laid
and stoned
and staid
old tourists
who keep coming
back to the same place
year after year
in the same
bathing suit.
Not much about life
is resolved,
but agreement as
to present weather conditions
about which any gone-blind
seagull
knows more.
maybe some beauty
in it all

EDWIN RILEY

WEDNESDAY

READING BY
EDWIN RILEY APRIL 6

8:00 p.m.

OPEN MIKE 9:00

PERFORMANCE PIECE AT 8:30. DON'T BE LATE.

READINGS FROM CONFRONT REALITY.You may be salad. and BURST OUT IN PARADISE.

1447 WASHINGTON STREET

1447 WASHINGTON STREET

Poetry reading at the iconic Cameo Theater
in Miami Beach, FL.

164

The Independent

Florida Alligator

THURSDAY
NOV. 7, 1974
VOL. 67, NO. 34

Published by Campus Communications Inc., Gainesville, Florida. Not officially associated with the University of Florida

Page 4, The Independent Florida Alligator, Thursday, November 7, 1974

'Beat' class via phone to Frisco

By CATHY CALLAHAN
Alligator Staff Writer

Lawrence Ferlinghetti questioned

TELE-LECTURE   photo by rick rosen
contemporary poet Lawrence Ferlinghetti chats with an English class via tele-lecture

Do you hear us? You are talking to the class now Mr. Ferlinghetti.

"Well I'm feeling pretty classy."

Everyone in the class says "Hi" in unison.

"Yea, I'm feelin' pretty high too."

LAWRENCE FERLINGHETTI, beat poet of the San Francisco Renaissance is talking to Ed Riley and David Robmann's "Literature of the Beats" class—over the telephone. The phone is attached to the tele-lecture system which amplifies his voice and allows students to question him with a microphone.

"Mr. Ferlinghetti, are you working on something now—another book?"

"No, I'm working on rolling a joint. I'm also doing something like serious creative activity. But I'm not saying the most important things—Howard Odum [of UF Department of Design's it. Why are you making long distance calls to me when the most important people are in your own backyard? Why don't you get Odum to talk to your class?"

FERLINGHETTI speaks from his San Francisco Bookstore, City Lights Publishing house. It's a place where people gather to read and talk, a place Ferlinghetti always wanted to have.

Ferlinghetti knows a lot about Florida. He talks very little about his poetry. This is because he pictures the poet as a transmitter of ideas—a consciousness-raiser. He believes poetry and commitment and politics go together. The poet should be involved in change.

"Did you know that the production of oranges is an energy loss to the state of Florida? Florida is pumping a lot of petroleum fertilizer into soil—the soil is not there—it's oil fertilizer. And the top of the tree is putting forth little orange petroleum products," he says.

"You people in Florida are getting ripped off and you don't even know it. I get the feeling you are all living in lotus land down there. You should get in touch with the Florida Caring Capacity Committee of the Legislature. They will tell you about the rape of Florida," Ferlinghetti says.

"I believe that industrial civilization will come to an end by the year 2,000. People don't believe this because of their own vested interests. You people in Gainesville feel you can have two cars in your garage and commute to class every day—well that will soon be over."

A student asks Ferlinghetti if he has anything positive to say—if he sees any optimistic signs.

"THE DEMOCRATS won," he responds. "Well—uh—I think it's good that thinkers like Howard Odum are trying to get politicians and businessmen to stop their folly. I am optimistic that things are not going on the way they were."

"The energy commission's report 'Energy and State Government' begins by saying all of human problems are vested in consciousness."

Ferlinghetti continues, "Buddhism or any religion is an attempt at raising consciousness. I'm interested in Buddhism because Christianity is not saying anything. Tibetan and Zen Buddhism are saying more than Christianity—especially out here. I talk about that in the poem "Crucifixion" which is in "Coney Island of the Mind."

(See 'Beat' page five)

Beat
(From page four)

ANOTHER STUDENT asks, "Do you think we need religion at all—why is it important?"

"I think you need to hear as much as you can from all directions. Do you want to go into a dark room with your ears stopped? We can go together," he laughs.

"In the '60's consciousness-expanding through the use of drugs took the place of religion. But it's all the same thing," Ferlinghetti said.

"BUT SOME people don't think so. That's why Leary is being held a political prisoner as much as anyone in the Gulag Archipelago," he added.

"Have you experimented with drugs," another student asks.

"Oh yea. There is a drug store on every corner. Who hasn't?"

ANOTHER STUDENT asks him about his poem "Lure is No Stone on the Moon."

Ferlinghetti responds, "Oh, that was pure ephemera. I wrote it before breakfast one morning—I think there were a few greens on the table that got swept into the coffee."

Someone asks him about the poem "I Am Waiting," in which he talks about the withering of governments and anarchy.

"It would be nice if we could make the world safe for anarchy. But Herbert Marcuse in "Eros and Civilization" explains that Eros is instinctual and that Civilization imposes restraints on eros."

"How strongly do you feel connected to the so-called beat movement?" someone asked.

"The press made up that term, or picked up on that term. The moon has no name but we call it the moon."

Another student asked, "If you feel so strongly about the end of civilization what are you doing about it?"

"I'm talking to you. That's my field."

Conference call with Lawrence Ferlinghetti,
father of the Beat generation.
*Credited to **The Independent Florida Alligator**.*

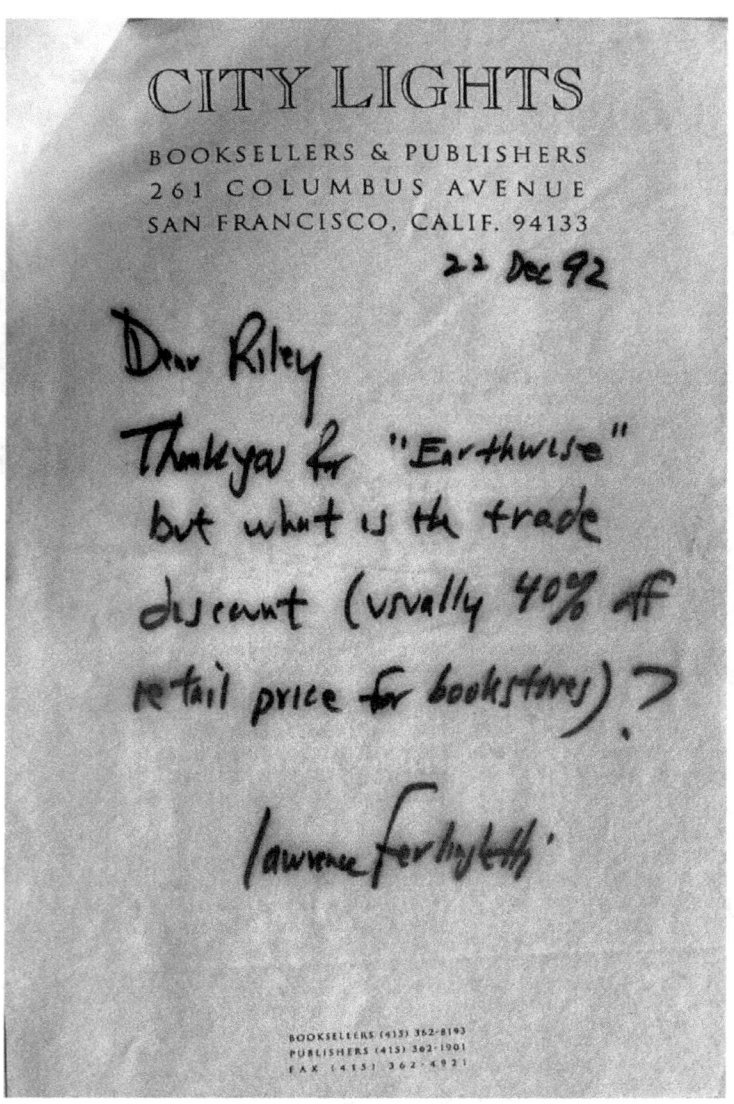

CITY LIGHTS

BOOKSELLERS & PUBLISHERS
261 COLUMBUS AVENUE
SAN FRANCISCO, CALIF. 94133

22 Dec 92

Dear Riley

Thankyou for "Earthwise"
but what is the trade
discount (usually 40% off
retail price for bookstores)?

Lawrence Ferlinghetti

BOOKSELLERS (415) 362-8193
PUBLISHERS (415) 362-1901
FAX (415) 362-4921

*Note from Lawrence Ferlinghetti,
written on City Lights letterhead, 1992.*

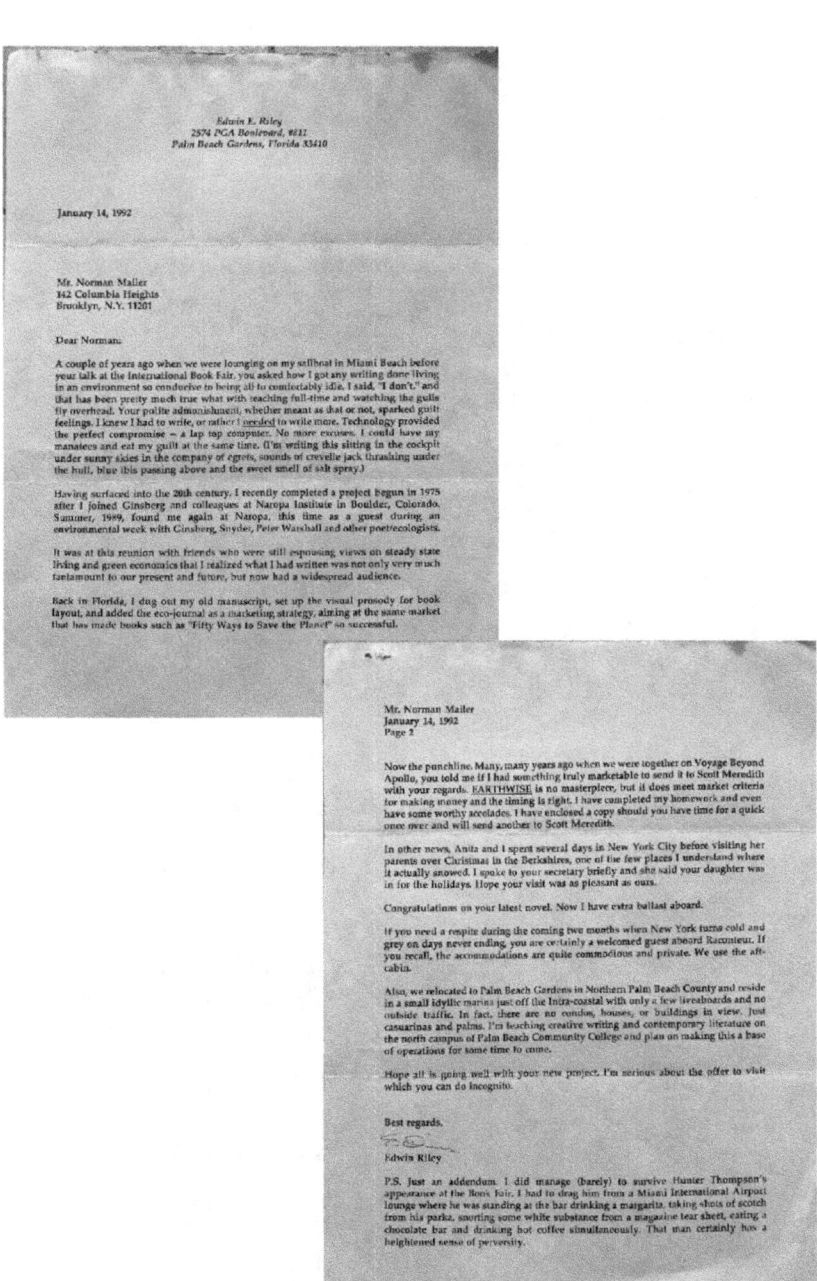

Letter to Norman Mailer, January 14, 1992.

25 June 1992

Dear Edwin,

I can see I let you down. The date on your letter is 14
January and all I can say is it fell to the bottom of a barrel
and I never got energetic enough to answer all the letters in
the barrel, and there you were, trapped down there and never
even being able to know what my reaction was to what you'd
written. By now, I guess you've heard from Scott Meredith and
if I'd heard in time, I'd have told you not to send it because
they charge a fee for reading and giving an evaluation. You
can't just send them a book unless it's properly presented. So
all I can say is, my apologies. You treated me real well down
in Miami and I didn't reciprocate appropriately.

Cheers,

Norman Mailer

28 October 1992

Dear Edwin Riley,

I can't answer your letter properly. I've been in Russia
and am off again to Moscow in two days. Won't be back for
months. So this is more to acknowledge your letter than to
answer it. All I can say is--sincerely, as they say on the
black market--

Yours, cheers,

PS. I've checked my dates and I won't be in new York on
December 5 and 6 but maybe we can hook up on your next visit.
I hope things go well and I'm glad Scott Meredith didn't charge
you.

Norman Mailer's Replies, 1992.

168

PBG Lifestyle Magazine.

He's Followed His Dreams In Life Rich With Variety

Learning Wonder Is Riley's Formula

Taking RISKS and following one's dreams is a formula for discovering the meaning of "wonder."

170

Holistic healer, student of life finds answers in remote Mexico

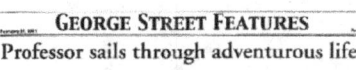

GEORGE STREET FEATURES

Professor sails through adventurous life

Communication professor Dr. Edwin Riley offers unique alternatives to teaching, medicine and life

Dr. Edwin Riley: 'A person needs calmness and balance'

Stress Rx
with Dr. Edwin Riley

Join us each issue as Dr. Edwin Riley offers advice on how to deal with today's stress.

Healing, Teaching, and Living Freely
The Art of an Unconventional Life.

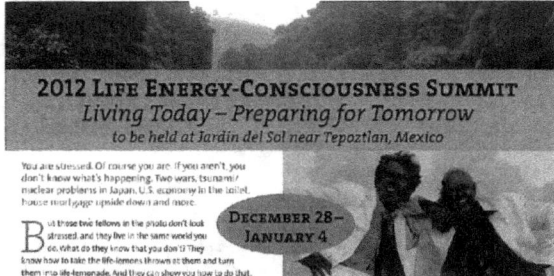

2012 LIFE ENERGY-CONSCIOUSNESS SUMMIT
Living Today – Preparing for Tomorrow
to be held at Jardin del Sol near Tepoztlan, Mexico

You are stressed. Of course you are. If you aren't you don't know what's happening. Two wars, tsunami/nuclear problems in Japan, U.S. economy in the toilet, house mortgage upside down and more.

DECEMBER 28– JANUARY 4

But these two fellows in the photo don't look stressed and they live in the same world you do. What do they know that you don't? They know how to take the life-lemons thrown at them and turn them into life-lemonade. And they can show you how to do that. They can show you how to use your brain, body and belly to change your outlook and live a fuller, happier life. So, who are these guys and how can they provide such dramatic changes?

These guys are Viktoras Kulvinkas on the left, and Dr. Edwin Riley on the right. Edwin is a pioneer in Mind/Body Medicine and Stress Reduction and Viktoras is the co-founder of Hippocrates Health Institute and a world renowned raw food expert.

Recent books by the pair are *Stress Rx: 103 Prescriptions for Overcoming Stress and Achieving Lifelong Happiness* by Dr. Riley and *Survival in the 21st Century* by Rev Kulvinkas.

Viktoras and Edwin will lead the Summit. Assisting Edwin and Viktoras will be Civil Rights Activist and Hall of Fame Comedian Dick Gregory, Eddie Brill, Comedian and Writer on the David Letterman show for 16 years, and many vocal musicians, poets and puppeteers.

The entire week will be filmed as a historical documentary by noted Filmmaker Tahoga "Yogi" Ruga, a Fellini-trained filmmaker

and Director of a soon-to-be released Italian documentary film on Fellini's life. She also produced a documentary interpreting the Mayan Calendar and its significance as prophecy revealed through hieroglyphics. The movie will be co-produced by Dr. Edwin Riley and Viktoras Kulvinkas.

This history making event, subtitled, "Living Today – Preparing for Tomorrow," can accept only 150 students. It will be held at Jardin del Sol near Tepoztlan, Mexico. The location is considered by Mexicans to be the spot on the earth with the highest vibrational energy and is often referred to as "The Sacred Valley."

A portion of the Summit proceeds will go to support sustain-our education at a holistic school and orphanage near Santo Domingo, Mexico.

To register for this event and download a day-by-day program, go to www.funandblisa.org.

TAKE IT EASY!
A review of *Stress Rx: 103 Prescriptions for Overcoming Stress and Achieving Lifelong Happiness* by Edwin Riley, Ph.D.
By Hulu B. Keller

With the foreboding sense of uncertainty and fear generated in by the recession, many are stressed and face crises at work, home and in their relationships. Society is filled with stressed-out individuals and no one is immune; stress is an equal-opportunity condition. While some handle mental tension better than others, stress is still a part of most people's lives. In his newly released book, *Stress Rx: 103 Prescriptions for Overcoming Stress and Achieving Lifelong Happiness*, Dr. Edwin Riley offers remedies in an easy to understand and interactive format while guiding individuals to take personal responsibility for the stress in their lives. For those who don't know how deal with stress effectively, Stress Rx offers effective coping skills, relaxation techniques and breathing and meditation exercises helping to alleviate negative reactions to the mental and emotional strains of life.

The buddha said, "Do not dwell in the past, do not dream of the future. Concentrate the mind on the present moment." In other words, yesterday is a cashed check; tomorrow is a promissory note; now is the only cash on hand. People beat themselves up thinking of all the poor choices they made because they are attached to and how difficulty letting go of the past. Regrets and guilt about things done or not done plague most people. It is almost impossible to move forward when mired with worry about what might happen in the future. There is nothing that can change the past and the future does not exist yet. The critical time is now.

In *Stress Rx* Dr. Riley describes how constant anxiety and the cumulative effects of long term stress can severely affect our life. "Our stress response is triggered by the mind; fearful or worrisome thoughts that produce a chemical reaction in the body. When this *fight-or-flight* response is invoked by a situation we see as threatening, the hormones cortisol and epinephrine, also known as adrenaline, are released into the blood-stream. When this happens, the heart beats faster, blood pressure soars, the muscles tense and the extremities might feel cold and clammy," he says. Some symptoms of harboring stress are obsessive thought patterns, all kinds of compulsive behavior towards sex, drugs, eating and drinking, and panic attacks, which feel like heart attack symptoms such as chest pains, rapid heartbeat, throat constriction,

dizziness, trembling and shaking. These stress symptoms are often followed by feelings of despair, depression and fear that it might occur again. As Dr. Brian Clement states in the foreword to Dr. Riley's book, "there is no better way to devastate your immune system than to have gnawing, destructive thoughts pervade your consciousness."

Medical experts say that between 80-95% of illness today is illness related. Stress can cause nausea, migraine, insomnia, and if prolonged, serious illness and disease. *Stress Rx* contains many suggestions on how to better handle almost any life situation such as:

Know that it is okay to cry, let the tears flow; don't keep them bottled up.

Pay close attention to gut feelings and physical symptoms like sharp pain, twinges, constipation, and trembling eyelids, cheeks and hands.

Chronic colds, sinus infections and rashes are all signs that something is out of balance.

When feeling attacked with aggressive or hostile behavior, don't take it personally; instead practice patience and understanding. You are the target of someone else's anger. Their behavior is a reflection of their inability to handle the stress in their lives.

Be mindful of your thoughts and reactions. It is amazing how a smile and a positive attitude quickly diffuse Cont'd on page 61

Review of *Stress RX*, cont'd from p.55
a negative situation.

Stress triggers eating disorders and phobias for every kind of life situation such as fear of illness, rejection, accidents, death, unfaithfulness, success, failure, being alone—the list is endless.

Virtually any form of exercise can decrease the production of stress hormones and counteract the body's natural stress response. Lack of exercise creates all kinds of physical havoc in the body. The ancient art of Tai Chi and yoga are non-competitive exercises using gentle stretching and flowing movements to reduce stress and improve agility.

Research has shown that music has a profound healing effect on the body and psyche. Hospitals are beginning to use music therapy to help with pain management and to ward off depression and anxiety.

These and other tips in *Stress Rx* teach those feeling any level of stress how to release and overcome the accumulated effects which can be damaging to the body and mind. *Stress Rx* is now available at the Hippocrates Store and via mail-order.

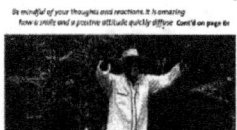

Dreamers create reality and new ideas are limitless when you dare to be yourself.

Kevin Patrick Greene and crew onboard Physalia.

KEVIN PATRICK GREENE
Irish To The Core

"Sometimes you've just got to make a decision."
— from the Captain's Log

Kevin Patrick Greene didn't stand a chance. Born on St. Patrick's Day with a six-pack of Guinness in his cradle, he was destined to drink excessively. Things got so out of hand for a while that I would disconnect my phone at night. This came after a 2 a.m. cry for help.

Kevin said he was being held hostage at gunpoint in a Coconut Grove smuggler's home.

After an alleged disagreement, he had been locked in a bedroom with bars on the windows. I found it strange they left him with a phone.

Kevin pleaded for my assistance, saying he didn't want police involved.

"If I'm not back in 30 minutes, call the cops," I told my girlfriend, climbing reluctantly from the sailboat's comfortable v-berth.

Sometimes we stayed at her apartment, other nights on the boat. She was threatening more apartment time until we pulled the phone plug.

This was the third such call in a month. The other two originated from the emergency room at Mercy Hospital.

Once, Kevin passed out riding his bicycle and ended up splattered on Biscayne Boulevard.

Next time, he drove off a pier at Dinner Key Marina, striking his head on a dock box before plunging into the water. He ignored my semi-serious suggestion to trade his bike in for a three-wheeler.

It was getting bad. The emergency room staff now knew him on sight. He was becoming a "regular."

A happy drunk, Kevin glanced down at the prescription as he came through the double doors into the waiting room.

"Tylenol Three," he scoffed, "this won't do."

Crumpling the prescription into a ball that he hurled across the room, missing the trash container by yards, he marched defiantly back through the double doors, loudly demanding stronger drugs.

Two orderlies, one on each arm, delivered Kevin. "Get your buddy out of here or we're calling the police."

No surprise to hear no ruckus that night I went to his rescue, driving down the darkened street. Kevin's car was not in the drive.

I drove back to the marina, now fully awake, adrenaline pumped. Calling his house, Kevin answered the phone. He was half asleep.

"Thought you were being held prisoner," I blurted, not totally jubilant to discover he was safe in bed.

"Tell you about it tomorrow," he said.

"Got to get some sleep."

His later explanation never made sense. That's when I decided to unplug the phone.

A week later Kevin called. His brother-in-law, an Englishman Kevin never got along with, had died. A perpetual drunk who kept a jug of wine under his bed for middle of the night shots in the dark, his liver finally succumbed to abuse.

His body was to be cremated, and Kevin's sister asked if we could do a burial off my sailboat at sea. She got seasick, so she would hold a memorial service ashore simultaneously.

Physalia had starter problems.

"Give me some money and we'll rent a boat," Kevin told his sister.

I drove my girlfriend's Toyota hatchback over to Kevin's mother's house where he and his sister were living.

She was standing in the doorway as Kevin jumped in the front seat, tossed the cardboard box containing his brother-in-law's remains onto the back seat, and grinning ear to ear waved forty dollars in my face.

"Beer money," he chimed. "Dirty Nelly's in Ft. Lauderdale, here we come."

The plan was simple. We would dispose of the remains on an outgoing tide from Bill Bagg's park at the tip of Key Biscayne. High tide wasn't until early evening.

Tommy Benson was a fun-loving guy and night bartender living in Lauderdale. We decided to take him along.

The day was hot and muggy, 90 degrees in the shade with 99 percent humidity. Tommy was kicked back in his air-conditioned apartment watching cartoons. He was game to go, but wanted to wait for his girlfriend, a nurse, to go with us. She would be home in 30 minutes.

Opening a round of beers, we talked guy talk as we waited.

"Kevin's brother-in-law is in the car," I said about 25 minutes later.

"You've got to be kidding," Tommy said. "Ask him in. He must be roasting out there. It's hotter than hell today."

"Really, no problem," Kevin said.

"The heat won't bother him."

Sarah arrived at that moment. "We should go now," Tommy said, explaining that Kevin's brother-in-law was waiting in the car. Sarah gave us all a look of disapproval. "Why didn't you ask him in?" she queried.

"The heat will kill him."

Kevin and I cracked up, doubling with laughter.

"I don't see what is so funny," she chided. "He must be toasted by now."

As Tommy and Sarah prepared to get in the car, they were perplexed, wanting to know about the brother-in-law.

"There," Kevin said, pointing to the box. "Told you the heat wouldn't bother him."

Tommy jumped back from the car. "I'm not getting in there with him," he screamed.

"He won't bite," I said, picking up the box and tossing it behind the seat into the hatchback.

Drinking beer at Dirty Nelly's can be a professional undertaking. By the time I dropped Kevin off, it was dark, and Bill was still in the box.

"You've gotta keep him until tomorrow," Kevin said, explaining he couldn't risk his sister finding out.

Not too fond of the idea, it didn't seem as if l had a choice.

Anita was waiting to go grocery shopping when I got to her apartment. She knew my plans for the day, but it was not discussed until the bag boy opened the hatchback to load the groceries.

Anita blanched, pointing a stiff index finger at Bill-in-a-box. "Is that whom I think it is," she questioned irritatingly.

I nodded.

The bag boy was perplexed but sensed something foul. "That's his friend's brother-in-law in that box," she declared.

The kid stepped back several feet. "Load them yourselves," he said, "I'm getting out of here. Too weird for me."

"He's right," Anita agreed.

"I don't want him in my car overnight."

"Great," I said, "we'll take him in the house."

"NO WAY! Just make sure he's gone tomorrow," she conceded.

As we had planned, I picked Kevin up and headed toward the tollgate at the entrance to Key Biscayne. The plan was the same. We would have a brief beer drinking ceremony and release Bill's ashes into Biscayne Bay, bound for the Atlantic on an outgoing tide.

Kevin was holding the box in his lap. Made of cardboard about the size of Girl Scout cookies, the charred remains were in a plastic bag with a twist wrap.

Just as we topped the high span bridge, Kevin hurled the box out the window and into the bay.

"What'd you do that for," I asked, a bit appalled at his irreverence.

Kevin looked at me in his Irish smiling innocence.

"Sometimes you've just got to make a decision."

We were both silent for a moment.

"Now let's go have a beer," Kevin said. "I'm buying."

*The ego-driven belief is that we are solid physical "matter,"
rather than makeup on empty space.*

MUSINGS ON ORGANIZED RELIGION AND FOMENT

"If we are evolving, then so must our God."
— from the Captain's Log

L ife is peculiar. No doubt about it. Better off not trying to figure out answers you'll never get. Like communicating with God. Once you think you have a handle on the conversation, it changes.

As well it should.

If you accept that we, as human beings, are constantly evolving, and that change is inevitable, then we must accept that our notion of divinity will change also.

Fundamentalists get knee-jerk crazy to hear this kind of logic. Prone to stand still, steeped in dogma, fear holds them steadfast to a belief system that has been spoon-fed like a blue plate special.

Never made sense to me. If the only thing constant is change, then our views of who God is must be changing also, realigning with our personal growth, our evolution. Especially if we are willing to become more conscious individuals, pioneers in this cosmic soup we all share as ingredients.

What this really means is no one can tell us about God except God. And we are constantly being updated, like computer software, with every breath.

I consider myself a spiritual being in a physical body, searching for meaningfulness in life.

My upbringing was in the Methodist church. Sunday school and church most Sundays were parentally required.

Mostly, I liked the music. The rest resonated gibberish. In the tenth grade, I started asking hard questions no one wanted to hear, much less venture an answer.

For a year, no one would teach our Sunday school class.

We sat there for an hour telling jokes and shooting the shit.

For all practical purposes, we had been "retired" early.

No one forces Sunday school attendance once you reach a certain age.

We had almost arrived, just got early release.

Carl Clary was the minister then.

Every summer we had beach retreats to Garden City.

David Graham always carried a fifth of bourbon in his knapsack.

Sandy Hudson repeatedly told on him.

His breath breathing fire, David denied the charges.

Carl was an unhappy camper. Especially the night Snooky, my roommate, was thrown in jail. He had gotten drunk at the bowery in Myrtle Beach. They allowed him one call. He called me with everyone in the church beach house looking on.

I pretended everything was okay, told Carl the minister that Snooky was visiting a friend overnight, and gathered all the guys upstairs to shell out bail money.

Wisely, and much to his credit, Carl joined his wife in prayerful sleep. He didn't lose his cool until two nights later when we tossed a large package of super-powerful fireworks into their room at 3 a.m.

Careening out of deep sleep, and obviously having reached his compassionate and understanding limit, he slammed the screen porch door ripping the hinges screaming obscenities.

Not a minister anymore, he was a bounty hunter. Shortly afterwards, he transferred to another church.

I'm a firm believer that religious fervor can be the deadliest of sins. How Jim and Tammy Faye Bakker pulled off their monumental scam perplexes. There is a long and short list of Elmer Gantry's. In hard times, they seem to proliferate, feeding like piranhas on insecure and gullible masses.

If I have a special pet peeve, organized religion gets my biggest vote.

Prayer is powerful. No doubt about it.

Studies prove it works. Folks who don't believe in palm trees get better when others pray for them.

Putting money into coffers out of fear, because someone else, another human being, is playing omnipotent, omniscient, and omnipresent, is a seriously rude and cruel joke.

They pass "Stop," go straight to hell in my monopoly book.

Again, like a psalms refrain, I believe if we are willing to admit we are evolving, then our thought processes have to evolve too.

I liked Carl Clary. He was a good, genuine, honest man, filled with integrity and commitment to something he truly believed in. As far as we go in this life, that's about all one can ask of another.

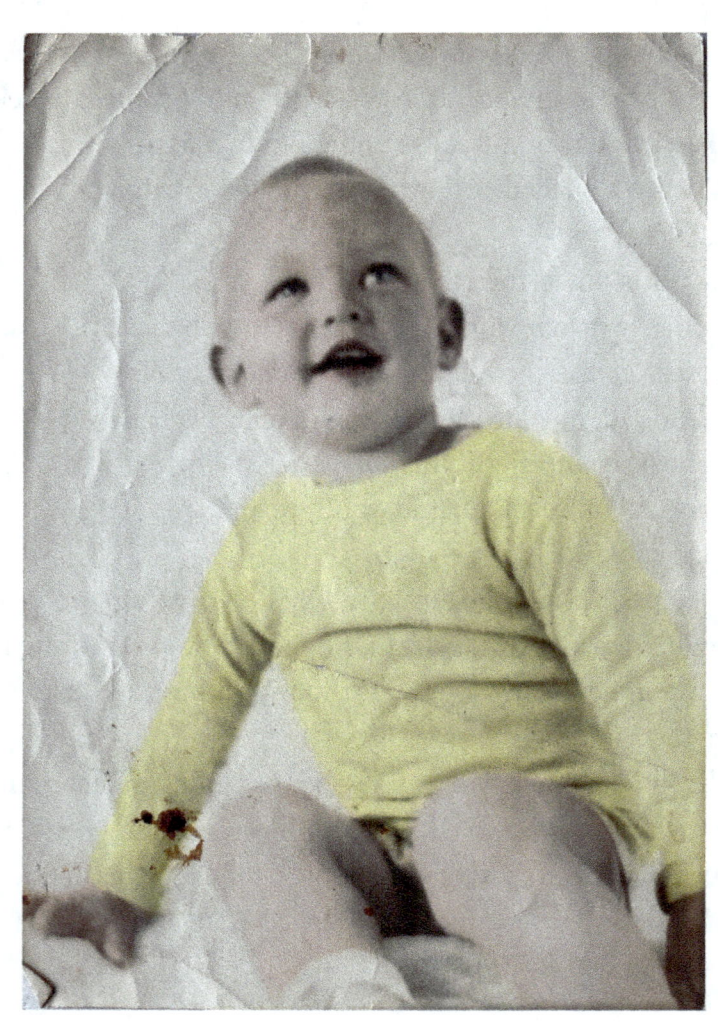

What the hell did I get myself into?

COMING INTO THIS WORLD

"I arrived under protest—with forceps and ether."
— from the Captain's Log

My birthing must have been horrendous. I don't remember. At least, not in my limited, day to day thinking mind.

All life experience is stored in a brain cell vault for posterity.

Mother remembers quite vividly.

I was pulled through her womb to freedom with forceps.

An indentation on the right side of my skull serves as a visual reminder.

Being first born, Mother was anxious.

A rather generous child in petite surroundings, eight pounds and six ounces, she resorted to what most women do under similar circumstances: panic.

She called Dad.

An ultimatum was decreed. Get the goddamn doctor, Dr. Dillard, to do something.

Mother is still alive, so I get firsthand remembrances.

The way she tells it, no wonder I have been plagued my lifetime with anxiety.

She was maxed out.

Brought me into this world on a bed of hot emotional nails.

Best she recalls, anesthesia included ether.

Everything else she could muster.

Funny thing is, she seldom drinks. And when she does, it's a small glass of the worst wine. Her penance.

185

My theory is, she so overdosed on my birth that she is afraid to venture further than her diet cola shelf.

No wonder I dwell in ethereal space.

Seems labor pains got so bad, at least in her way of thinking, that Dad called Dr. Dillard at home, threatening to break his neck if he didn't show up soon at the hospital.

According to Mother's story, which is always a bit circumspect, he arrived in time to declare that a cesarean section would have been appropriate.

Instead, he grabbed me, probably dragging and reluctant to leave a warm and fuzzy place, with what amounts to hard metal tweezers, and pulled me into the real world.

I've never fully recovered.

Here's looking at you, kid.

ON WRITING AND FEELING GOOD

"We are writers in our own time. Now is my time."
— from the Captain's Log

The more I write, the better I feel. If we are meant to say things other people feel, yet can't express, it is a duty, an obligation, maybe more a veritable compulsion, to write.

I don't understand it. What I do know is that I have resisted this impulse for a lifetime. Sure, I worked as a journalist. This has parameters, limits to growth, expression, and freedom. That's why I left.

Walked out the newsroom door.

Now I'm back with a vengeance. Sometimes we must marinate. Let juices flow to the surface.

We are writers in our own time. Now is my time. I am serene enough to sit, patient enough to reflect.

In my journey, I learned to listen to the wind.

Sailing taught me patience.

I've been writing like a machine gone berserk.

Something kicked in.

Maybe it is my freedom.

I'm sitting here in Islamorada, Florida, looking out over the ocean, and I feel the swell of sea and sensuality.

People tell me atmosphere doesn't matter.

Maybe not to them.

To me it matters.

I know what makes me tick.

Fuck those who tell me otherwise.

I can't work or live in a vacuum.

Certainly, I would survive given circumstances.

We rise to the occasion, usually minimally.

I produce when I am alive. Mostly I write sober. We all know the stories about writers.

They are drinkers. Nothing to argue there. Altered states of consciousness often promote creativity.

I've been there; will go again.

Alcohol creates heat. We burn layers of karma and leave a soliloquy wake.

No excuses anymore. No promises either.

Maybe songster Jimmy Buffet says it best,

"Life is just a tire swing."

Another brief career as a model in Miami Beach.
Living life is a continuous evolution.

J.W. ALLEN AND WEED GARDENS

"I don't want to be a spoke on a wheel."
— from the Captain's Log

Love is not forever. Like perennials, some relationships fade, then come back again. Others simply perish.

Lots of conditions govern outcomes. Farmers know this probably better than anyone.

Planting seeds doesn't guarantee groceries.

Too much heat; too little.

Not enough nurturing, too much.

All factors in farming, and love.

What we want, we may not get. Or vice-versa

Then there is pre-meditated love. J.W. Allen was guilty in the first degree. We met working at the Wilmington, N.C. newspaper, both age twenty, both married.

My second newspaper job, I wrote most city and county government news. He had switched from writing for a small upstate weekly to an advertising training program.

Like two rascally peas in a combustible pod, we were instant friends.

"Today's my wedding anniversary," he shared, standing in a narrow corridor as he filed advertising copy. We had introduced ourselves just moments earlier.

"Congratulations," I offered, politely.

For J.W., a free spirit of the highest caliber, his first wedding anniversary meant freedom.

He had agreed to marry Ann, a nurse, in a weak moment. On a double date, the other couple, professing their love, decided on that evening's whim to marry, suggesting J.W. and Ann do likewise.

Ann encouraged the spontaneous union. J.W. consented but only if it lasted for a year.

Cut from a different cloth, usually limited to madmen and poets, J.W. had been expelled from high school in Raleigh two weeks before graduation.

He had gotten in trouble before for wearing a bed sheet and sandals to class. This was his "philosophy uniform."

He dressed this way when he sat beneath an oak tree in the nearby cemetery and read excerpts from Sartre to his small following.

An English teacher kicked him out for stating his views in a semester composition, especially offended by the reference to her as a "pagan of corporate society."

She took J.W. to task for being an "enemy of the state," "communist," and "a heretic."

J.W. packed his bongos, moved to the remote coastal town of Belhaven and took up writing for the hamlet's weekly.

Bored and naive, that's when he met Ann, got married on the spur of a moment, and moved to Wilmington, signing up for the six-year advertising training program.

A year had passed. A deal was a deal, J.W. believed.

Tonight, he would pack his bags and move out of the house they rented on Wrightsville Beach.

"How'd it go?" I asked him the next day.

J.W. was more than mildly disappointed. He had been attached for a year to an entirely different outcome.

"Not too well," he began.

"She was waiting in a sexy nightgown with flowers and champagne when I got home. She asked me if I knew what day it was. I said, 'Sure. A year is up. I'm going to pack my bags after we drink the champagne to celebrate.'"

Ann threatened suicide. This took J.W. off guard. He consented to stay until he could figure out a solution.

Two kids and ten years later, he finally walked out.

J.W. is not an unkind soul. Quite the contrary.

He just never left childhood.

Once they rented a nice home in an upscale neighborhood next to a church. J.W. took pride in his weed garden. Much to the neighbor's chagrin, he would water his weeds like they were prized flowers.

The minister was delegated to reason with J.W.

Maybe he could save his soul in the process.

As one might conclude, J.W. wasn't interested in having his soul tampered with. In fact, he was a devout agnostic.

On the minister's third attempt to get into J.W.'s home for conversation and deliberation, J.W. swung the front door wide open, stark naked, with a martini in one hand.

The minister fled.

Freedom is contagious.

Perhaps that is why I was so drawn to J.W. He was an inspiration to the individual spirit, much to our wives' dismay.

We fed off each other.

All it took was benign conversation to get us going. They came over for dinner one night; someone suggested we all go to a movie.

J.W. recalled the beach scene in the movie *From Here to Eternity*. Then I began. Musings on coastal smells, sea oats, wave noises, and body surfing.

"We've got to see the beach," we said, practically in unison, as if it was just around the corner, rather than 220 miles. It was getting late. We could make it before sunrise.

Both wives gave us that "I can't believe this is happening again" look of disapproval and resignation.

I grabbed my guitar, we dropped the top on my Austin Healey sports car, swung by J.W.'s for his bongos, bought a six-pack of beer, and drove off into the Raleigh, N.C., night bound for Myrtle Beach, S.C.

We were stretched out on lounge chairs at the motel swimming pool when the sun came up. Like two poets in ecstasy, we celebrated sunrise with words, exchanging our own vernacular take, and did the same covering all the senses in colorful adjectives for an hour.

I sang *House of the Rising Sun* to J.W.'s accompaniment on his bongos. Then we got in the Austin Healey and drove back home.

J.W. was more "off the wall" than myself. Except for his day job at the newspaper selling advertising, he would change lifestyles every six months like clockwork.

Once, he decided to become a photographer. To J.W., this meant buying every piece of equipment on the market and renting a home suitable for setting up a darkroom. When the novelty waned, he would move on to something else.

Like the time he decided to become a fly fisherman and country gentleman. Not satisfied with just finding a home outside town, he wanted it to "look the part," like searching for a movie set.

Not put off by the old home's warped floors and lack of air conditioning, it had all the panache of a fisherman's shanty. And it had a pond.

Getting down the red clay road was messy and precarious. Rainy days the road was impossible to travel without getting stuck. J.W. didn't care. He bought a German shepherd, saying every fisherman needed a dog.

Dressed in hip waders and hat covered in fishing flies, he would wade into the pond with his dog. I never saw him catch a fish.

Because conditions were so awful, the ramshackle house, rutted clay road, gnats and hornets, he seldom received company.

Tired of the desolation, he moved back to town.

For the next six months, he would change out of his day job three-piece suit and cordovan shoes into blue jeans, working shirt, and sandals, and drink espresso at the Sidetrack, a hippie hangout in the warehouse district next to the casket company.

The Sidetrack was a calling card to folk singers that came to town on tour. Peter, Paul, and Mary arrived one night. So did Bob Dylan and Joan Baez. It was a hip scene. I would read poetry on open mic nights. If the audience approved, they would snap fingers. No one clapped. Not cool.

Hanging with J.W. fed my individual leanings. I never had been a joiner. Many people join out of peer pressure.

Several years later, I returned to college, earning a B.A. in journalism.

Moving to Orlando, Florida, I joined an advertising/public relations firm as chief copywriter.

As a way to network, they insisted I join a civic organization. The Winter Park Jaycees met for breakfast weekly near my home. As a lesser of evils, I figured early morning would get it over with. Besides, I needed to eat.

The guys liked me. I liked some of them too, but I didn't want to officially join. They kept pushing. I kept resisting, making lame excuses in the process.

One day the state Jaycee president came to breakfast. It was a big deal, members were being inducted. I sat at the head end of the runway connecting to the head table.

He started calling out names for new inductees to stand and take an oath to become a "spoke on a wheel." My name was called. I sat still. He called it again, looking down the long table, waiting for me to rise. All the others waited, too.

I didn't move.

The silence was palpable. In that eternal moment, I thought of J.W. He wouldn't have stood either. The reason was clear: neither of us are lemmings.

I just shook my head "no" until they gave up trying to pry me from the chair.

Some were openly angry. Others simply perplexed.

Surrounded by a group after the meeting, one asked the inevitable: "Why didn't you stand and take the oath?"

"I don't want to be a spoke on a wheel," I replied.

I was not invited back.

I hold no contempt for Jaycees or any civic organization. I simply don't fit.

Time is an illusion. Sublime or serene, the quality is orchestrated in circumstances. An orgasm can be fleeting or eternal depending on the situation. It is still an orgasm in space and time.

Like bird tracks in beach sand, we are only flickers in time and space. So why does all this happen? Who am I? What is my purpose?

Certainly, none of these questions answer being a spoke on a wheel of networking corporate pimps. Rather I am a blemish on the rump of a pelican in flight.

Should we continually make concessions to not soar, rather to stretch as if we as humans might fly?

Ramblings on the vagaries of our very existence take energy and courage. Much easier to stand unquestionably when summonsed than sit on ideals.

Which brings me back to J.W. Allen whose notion of a bonanza night out was to play his bongos sitting on the tarmac at the end of the airport runway.

Later in life, his six-month lifestyle change became camping. Now divorced, his weekend girlfriend found his innocence both charming and difficult. She couldn't quite grasp his compulsion to drive four hours out of the way to show me his new hunting knife.

What she failed to understand is that J.W. had missed out on childhood, so he was making up for time lost. His childhood was now.

Excitedly, we touched the knife blade, discussed its sharpness, held its sheath, and 30 minutes later there was nothing more to say. After all, it was just a knife.

Like the green flash of a Key West sunset, he was gone, heading for the campground and a new experience.

All too often we are held hostage by our expectations of what others would expect of us.

When this happens, we lose much more than just our identity. J.W. had his intact.

*Introducing Gonzo journalist Hunter S Thompson
before a packed audience in Miami.*

HUNTER S. THOMPSON
When The Going Gets Weird

"Serendipity is a wonderful law of nature.
Just keep the faith."
— from the Captain's Log

While teaching at Miami-Dade Community College, I was appointed to the International Book Fair's authors' committee. This is a huge November event drawing writers around the world.

As a committee, we usually met once a week at Mitch Kaplan's house.

The owner of the legendary independent Coral Gables bookstore *Books & Books*, famous for its eclectic offerings and weekly wine-and-cheese book readings, Mitch would host the authors' committee meetings, where we discussed themes and writers to invite.

I pushed for the nefarious gonzo journalist Hunter S. Thompson. Better recognized for his lunatic behavior than his actual talent, he nevertheless got religious-like endorsement with much fanfare from his dedicated readers.

Rightfully nervous, the committee was understandably reluctant about his presence. They nixed the idea.

Another year rolled around.

Again, I threw Hunter's name in the ring. His most celebrated book was the early seventies' *Fear and Loathing in Las Vegas*, a rambling LSD-generated odyssey.

Timing is everything. What he wrote back then was irreverent and funny. He took on Richard Nixon and other offensive establishment icons. As the saying goes, Thompson took no prisoners. Drugs were "in."

He touted them like cookies and milk.

Intentionally outrageous to the hilt as his trademark, Thompson spelled "trouble." He mumbled unintelligibly and incoherently when giving readings. Not all the time, just most.

Everyone we invited in 1988 was sane and talented. I argued for balance, someone off the wall. Most Beat writers had faded from public eye.

Hunter still had a large following with his *Rolling Stone* and *Playboy* magazine articles. Plus, he had written another book released in hardback.

Having run for sheriff in Woody Creek, Colorado, where he lived in isolation, had a reputation for firing guns at random, and indulged in hot tub and cocaine debauchery, Thompson upped his national profile when he almost won the race.

A reasonable choice based on his large magazine readership, as well as recent books, the committee relented with caution.

"He is all yours," they emphasized. "Sign him up, get him to the auditorium, introduce him, and keep trouble at bay."

Hunter's agency was William Morris, one of the world's largest, based in New York. Oddly enough, his agent was Betsy Berg, a friend of my wife's family. I didn't know this until contacting the agency to negotiate.

"Just make sure he is never out of your sight," Betsy warned. She was adamant and convincing. "Especially when you get to the airport. He will want to hit the bars."

Whether for reputation's sake or personal decadence, Thompson's contract had a clause calling for a bottle of scotch and ice at his side when he spoke.

Thompson was scheduled to speak in the main auditorium in downtown Miami on Tuesday evening.

The first sign of trouble came early that morning over National Public Radio. Hunter had shown up at the Ritz in New York two hours late for an appearance. Described as being out of control and unintelligible, he emptied the place when he began assembling a rifle on stage.

Worse news came late afternoon.

Hunter was missing.

His assigned escort had been given the slip.

No one knew his location.

Recalling my freelance starving days in the early seventies, I reflected, as I waited for news of his whereabouts, on how I had contracted with *Rolling Stone* magazine to write about spring break in Ft. Lauderdale.

Contacting the larger Northeast universities, I aligned with a fraternity. I planned to hang out as an observer, comparing modern rituals to those captured in the earlier spring break movie classic, *Where the Boys Are*.

Several untimely incidents got in the way.

Before heading south, the fraternity received several innocuous violations. The national chapter warned another infraction could close them down. They took it seriously.

According to George, my contact and a Greek frat president, he thought I wrote for *Time* magazine, not for liberal *Rolling Stone*.

Taking a vote behind closed doors, they decided not to let me stay and watch. Too dangerous, they felt, for the fraternity's tenuous future.

I was on the streets in Ft. Lauderdale.

Al Satterwhite, a prominent free-lance photographer assigned to cover the story showed, decided he couldn't wait for me to come up with an option, suggested we scrub the story, and headed back across state to Tampa.

Doing what most writers in similar situations do, I grabbed a cold beer and found a suitable perch on the Intracoastal for watching yachts and a spectacular sunset.

That's when I met Captain Dan, who lived on a sailboat docked at Pier 66. Owned by the Colgate toothpaste family, Dan was stocking the sailboat for a tiger-hunting trip to the Yucatán. He had a good yarn to weave and offered me a bunk for the night if I, in return, would drive him north to Pompano Beach to meet with his girlfriend.

Like most Hunter Thompson stories, this night took on legendary proportions. Without going into detail, Captain Dan and his girlfriend were on the outs.

I drove him to a bar.

She was there. With another man.

Captain Dan was not a happy captain.

Neither was the girlfriend, who accused him of spying on her. Sir Galahad, her escort, wanted to fight.

The night got old quick.

Being a natural-born pacifist, I retreated to a table of young women having just arrived from Ohio for spring break. Working on what most certainly would become monumental hangovers, they were chugging sweet, heavily liquored drinks laced with oriental umbrellas and plastic swordfish.

Regaling them with my plight as the ousted writer, I was invited to join the sorority.

Serendipity is a wonderful law of nature. Like the saying goes, when one door closes, another one opens. Just keep the faith. At that moment, my belief in synchronicity soared off the proverbial chart.

Finding a pay phone that I could hear from in the noisy bar, I called *Rolling Stone* editor Jann Wenner. "Change of story plans," I excitedly explained, asking him to locate the photographer and send him back.

Not all the girls were delighted with my male membership. Feeling physically and conversationally inhibited, I was permitted one night's stay, then sent packing.

Out on the street again, I bounced from place to place for several days, turning a potential debacle into adventure.

Lemons into lemonade.

Freelancing is a hard way to make a living. You're usually out of pocket, meaning you must cover expenses until reimbursed and paid for the story itself. Always taking weeks, and sometimes never, you still are faced with supporting a family and incoming bills.

Armed with notepads, I returned home to Cape Canaveral and sat at the typewriter. Jann Wenner had called several times, anxious for the article.

Back then, we wrote on manual or electric typewriters.

No faxes, everything was sent Federal Express.

I plodded on, put it together gonzo-style, and sent it packing. Weeks passed. No check.

Finally, I called Wenner.

"Sorry," he explained, "Hunter Thompson wrote an article too similar to yours. Bottom line is, we run 25,000 extra street copies when his name appears. Maybe next time. Good luck."

Irony is a strange bedfellow. Here I was, endorsing the lunatic writer who had picked my pocket unwittingly only 14 years earlier. And I was getting screwed again.

By 4:30 p.m., word had come down.

Intoxicated and paranoid, Hunter had managed to catch a flight back home to Woody Creek. He would be a no-show. Calling him personally after strong language with the agency, Hunter answered the phone.

Said he was sick and "snowed in." Weather reports confirmed heavy Colorado snow. Later, reports from his New York escort, given the slip, also confirmed a Hunter Thompson self-induced "snowstorm" of a different kind.

Promising to appear on Saturday, I hesitantly rescheduled, saying I would meet him as he came off the concourse.

Meanwhile, back in Miami, we alerted the media of his cancellation. We also ran off flyers and passed them out as people arrived for the evening's performance.

Not taking any chances for reasons to detour our route to campus, on Saturday afternoon I loaded a cooler with Hunter's favorite scotch, ice, beer, and limes into my 1972 VW Bug.

I waited for his arrival. Soon his scheduled flight disembarked. The line got slimmer. Next came flight attendants and captain. I was in disbelief.

Racing downstairs to luggage, thinking perhaps he had slipped my watchful eye, he was nowhere in sight.

Anxiously, I bounded back up to the concourse entrance, just in time to see the notorious Hunter S. Thompson, tall and gangly, ambling nonchalantly in my direction.

"I need a drink," he said, by way of introduction as we cordially shook hands.

"Got you covered," I said,

"Scotch and Beer are in the car, waiting."

Hunter was already headed to the bar.

"No, I want a margarita," he said, queuing up to the line.

I figured we had maybe 30 minutes lead-time.

A big sports bar, both televisions behind the bar were blaring a football game. Hunter strikes an unusual and diabolical pose.

Even in an airport bar, patrons cleared a path.

Waiting on his margarita, he had bought a coffee and chocolate-covered ice cream bar.

His conversation is more staccato than complete sentences, somewhat difficult to follow. He was talking small talk, mostly to himself, bits of chocolate hanging from his chin, sipping coffee and guzzling a margarita.

Usually tallest in a group, and pasty white compared to the Miami patrons, he struck a strange, out-of-sync pose.

His appearance was drawing attention.

Some patrons decided they were safer in leaving, especially after he pulled a magazine tear sheet from his jacket pocket, snorted the white substance, licked the full-color page, crumpled it into a ball, and tossed it in the wastebasket over the bartender's shoulder.

Miami International is generally 50 percent Latin Americans and 50 percent DEA agents. I figured it was time to leave. So did everyone else.

"Hunter, we've got to leave," I said.

"I want another margarita," he insisted.

I looked at the bartender.

"Can we possibly have a go cup?" I asked.

"NO PROBLEM," he anxiously volunteered.

Hunter had the times confused. He thought it was Tuesday. We were on Saturday.

He was to be on stage an hour earlier.

In the car, Hunter pulled out an envelope and began spooning the white substance into his nose, offering me some of his stash.

"No thanks," I refused. "I'm wired enough."

Hunter was paranoid by the time we arrived downtown, saying he couldn't walk down the auditorium aisle. He wanted to enter backstage. Someone had dropped the ball on his end.

They had forgotten his stage scotch and ice.

Hunter refused to budge. "It's in my contract," he screamed. "I'm not going on without it. And you have to sit on stage next to me," he said, his arm now around my shoulder.

Hunter Thompson fans are a restless, angry lot.

Many come for the antics; some join in.

Waiting for his scotch to arrive, I walked on stage to deliver my introduction. It was not a pretty sight. Only a few cared to listen. Others started chanting for Hunter.

Backstage, Hunter started lobbing curtain weights across the stage at me. I waved for him to come out, our two chairs center stage near the podium. He was shaking his head.

The crowd got louder. To hell with my introduction, I decided, walking over to Hunter, grabbing his arm, and pulling him beyond the stage curtain to the packed audience.

His scotch arrived as we sat down.

I poured him a glass on the rocks.

Unable to locate his sunglasses, he complained to the audience who accommodated by tossing sunglasses onto the stage.

I don't recall what he said that night.

I do remember though that his speech, usually garbled beyond interpretation, actually improved. Nobody else probably remembers what he had to say, either.

Quite a few got up from their seats and left well before the talk ended.

Later, he was asked to leave the hospitability room by the host after Hunter fired up a joint and passed it around to his student groupies.

A former friend, Richard Godwin, refused to visit with Hunter, suggesting I get him out of town as quickly as possible. My wife refused to let him stay on our sailboat for a couple of days even though he would have liked to.

I finally left him to his entourage of followers, destined for a late night of serious partying.

When I got to Hunter's hotel room at 7 a.m. the next morning, he was still awake, the bed unmade, reading the sports page and drinking a Heineken.

Cleaning the residue off the kitchen sink with his tongue, he put the remaining beers in both coat pockets as we left the hotel.

On the way to the airport, I handed him my worn paper-back copy of *Fear and Loathing in Las Vegas.*

"Usually I don't ask for autographs," I told him.

"But I don't think you'll be around much longer."

Hunter laughed, took the book, and inscribed:

"Edwin, thanks for getting me to the goddamn airport on time."
—Hunter S. Thompson.

Iced 'T'

Still cool to his long-time fans, a cold disappointment to others, Hunter Thompson sends audience walking.

KAREN SMITH
Metropolis analyst

"Where's my cigarettes? I just want to find my bag, it's got the whiskey in it. Jesus, I've been deprived of everything since I got here. I need ice."

After finally stumbling onto the stage an hour later for his rescheduled book fair appearance, Hunter Thompson seemed more concerned about maintaining his semi-coherent state than discussing anything other than the fact that he was "embarrassed by the Democrats' inability to field a candidate to beat Bush."

Together, those two themes dominated the evening and were apparently what a significant part of the audience wanted. With questions ricocheting back and forth between the drug-related and the politically motivated, there was little chance to steer the dialogue to other areas.

Of course with Thompson's continual slide into an incomprehensible slur and mumble, it's doubtful that it would have been of much value or interest anyway. It certainly couldn't have been more repetitious, however.

While large factions of the audience shouted out inanities relating mainly to drugs, exploiting the lack of structure during the "lecture," an equally large group of disillusioned baby boomers seemed anxious to relive their political activism in the past, or receive affirmation of their views from a former hero of their generation.

All in all, it became more of a Hunter Thompson fan

■ Hunter Thompson gets his much-needed ice from host Edwin Riley.

club meeting than any sort of genuine dialogue between writer and readers, with over half the audience walking out early on.

The seats vacated were an ironic symbol to those who had waited up to two hours for a chance to hear Thompson speak and belied the declarations that this was the most popular event of the fair. By the end, it was obvious that many people had found more entertaining ways to spend their Saturday night out.

While Thompson's appearance was generally a disappointment to those expecting the acid wit and humor so evident in his early books, such as *Fear and Loathing in Las Vegas*, he did have his occasional moments.

When asked what he thought about Dan Quayle, Thompson replied, "He's a silly little bastard who might be president. I don't mind him being a silly bas-

tard, but I do mind him being president."

He also claimed several times to have the name of Bush's girlfriend, but it was unclear whether he was serious or not.

When questioned about his views on the new drug laws, Thompson claimed he was a "dope fiend," although it was a "crippling way of life. I don't hurt anybody." On further questioning regarding his ability to write while high, though, he conceded that he "preferred good lines to good drugs."

This last comment led some to speculate on the possibility that his reputation may be at least partly hype. If that is the case, he kept up the act admirably, and he can probably rest assured that very few people in Miami would accuse him of being too sober, too often.

213

Cover photo shoot for my book "Confront Realty,"
taken at Coconuts on the Beach in Cocoa Beach, Florida.

THE GREAT OREO TRAGEDY

"Never can tell when the muse to write will strike."
— from the Captain's Log

Anita was young and appealingly sassy. Not a raving beauty, I found her sexy and seductive. A 19-year-old English student of mine at Miami-Dade Community College, she appeared late one afternoon on the dock at Monty Trainer's Restaurant where I lived on my sailboat *Physalia*.

For all practical purposes, she stayed for 17 years, even though we didn't marry for nearly five years.

Being 18 years older, I had reservations from the start. Not so much an age difference concern, more about what she might ultimately require of lifestyle.

Having already shifted careers from journalist to marketing to college professor, and divorced with two rapidly growing children, I had no intention of returning to a corporate world.

At least in the moment, I eschewed any notion of being trapped, whether in marriage, certainly not suburban living, or in some mundane job.

Teaching, I originally thought, was on the outskirts, permitting more freedom than other venues, a means to pay bills in a thought-provoking environment.

Later I learned otherwise. Years of self-inflicted obstinacy kept me from realizing the truth. Education today is a business with the same petty egos and lackluster that my other working environments offered. It shouldn't, and doesn't have to be that way, it just is.

I was operating under idealistic and romantic delusion.

The upside teaching attraction was independence and time off. In many ways, this holds up, depending on where you teach. I took summers off to sail and explore, gathering life experiences.

Dating a student can be tricky. As an authority figure, although I'm not certain whether the authority lies with the student or the professor, you come under scrutiny and ethics. Mostly, you are subject to envy and gossip.

The inference is you're having sex. Of course you're sleeping together. I suggested Anita drop my class and sign up with another instructor. This might reduce the chatter and ease my classroom discomfort.

Time passes. The semester ends with a minimum of fanfare. For the most part, at least on campus, we were discreet. Groping in movie theaters didn't count.

Once spring semester ended in May 1981, we headed south, sailing *Hawk's Charmel* to Key West. My 11-year-old son, Trey, accompanied us, along with "Christmas," an eight-month-old, energetic, pain-in-the-ass black Lab. Fearing my loss of freedom, I had given the dog to Anita the previous Christmas, hence her name, thinking she'd spend more time at her apartment.

Manipulation always, not sometimes, but ALWAYS comes back to haunt·. Sometimes it takes longer. Now mine is instant, like one-minute grits. Law of Karma.

What goes around comes around.

Later, "Christmas," along with Anita, who loved the dog dearly, would come live on *Physalia*. Christmas' revenge started immediately, chewing a corner off *Physalia*'s precious and prized teak railing.

I loved the dog, regardless, but my fondness never once diminished her mischievousness, which lasted her lifetime.

The summer game plan was sailing south to Key West, exploring islands along the way, then taking a road trip to Maine, hugging coastal back roads, discovering off-the-beaten-path fishing villages and uninhabited beaches.

We would divert to New York City, visit her parents, and then continue along coastal Maine, looking forward to lobster co-op dining. The route back home would extend through the Appalachians, through North Carolina, to Columbia, South Carolina and my parents, then back down the coast.

Camping would be primitive.

We bought one of those extraordinarily small orange pup tents that come in a zip-lock sized nylon bag, one plaid sleeping bag, and a kerosene lantern.

Unable to find kerosene, we slept in early darkness until we reached Cape Cod and drove past a hardware store selling kerosene. Opening the lantern eagerly that evening, we read the instructions which elaborately described how any brand of charcoal lighter fluid would work.

Having opted for a weekend date with my neighbor's niece instead of a camping trip that terminated my Boy Scout affiliation, I was reaping the loss of some basic outdoor skills.

Kerosene, I soon discovered, burns acrid and dirty, the very reason it is seldom used today. I guess manufacturers still call them kerosene lanterns for nostalgic reasons.

Before heading north, we stopped in Miami for Trey's plane ride back to Gainesville and provisioned the car with the usual necessities: a case of beer, Doritos, Oreo cookies, and Wheat Thins.

Now fully provisioned, we headed up A1A, stopping briefly in Cocoa Beach to buy a surfboard and boogie board. Figuring we were doing a coastal jaunt, this would provide us with much-needed exercise after so much sitting.

Anita was driving the next leg on Interstate 95 that took us around the prohibited coastal area north of Jacksonville.

Munching on an Oreo double creamer, I glanced over as she made a strange guttural sound. Her face was beet red, dripping black and white specks at the corner of her mouth, giving her the appearance of a rabid pug.

Hurtling up I-95 at 80 miles an hour, I swung into action, now aware she was choking.

Bending her forward as much as possible, considering she was seat-belted and driving, I whacked her sharply on the back. Pieces of Oreo double creamers spewed forth, covering the dashboard and windshield.

Still panicky, but able to breathe again, she took her foot from the accelerator and pulled onto the highway shoulder, thankful to be alive, toasting the moment with large gulps of spring water.

I always carry a journal with me. Especially on odysseys. Never can tell when the muse to write will strike. Always unpredictable. Always unexpected. I have discovered how important for a writer to capture "the moment" as it unfolds, never quite knowing how it will reveal itself in a literary sense. This time brought a lyric:

"I had to call her parents,
To tell them how she died,
She choked to death on an O-R-E-O
On I-95."

Anita didn't particularly like my flippancy. Neither did her father when I told him the story. A lack of spoken judgment in the magic of song lyrics, I shelved the episode until one night in late October when I awoke at 4 a.m., a stream of stanzas coursing through my head.

"Heading north on A-1-A
One bright and early morn,
We left behind the sailboats,
And early August storms."

"Boiled peanuts filled the cooler,
Beer was packed on ice,
Key West was in the distance,
Then Key Largo came in sight."

"We stopped around Miami,
For another case of Heineken,
Hit that old Grand Union,
For more Doritos and Wheat Thins."

"We had the traveling munchies,
Eating everything in sight,
When terror struck,
Her eyes got stuck,
And rolled back out of sight."

"We crossed that ole Georgia line
When everything went wrong,
The beer got warm; there was a storm,
By now the reefer was all gone."

"I thought it was my singing
That made her feel displeased,
When a pack of Oreo Double Creamers
Fell right across her knees."

"Her face got red,
I should have guessed,
That the lady was in distress
I asked what's wrong?
Looked what you've done,
Gone and made a mess."

"And when she didn't answer,
I slapped her on the back,
But it was too late,
She'd met her fate,
An Oreo attack."

(Chorus)
"I had to call her parents,
To tell them how she died,
She choked to death, on an Oreo,
On I-95"

"And Lord I felt so foolish
Standing in that booth,
But the culprit was an Oreo,
That robbed her of her youth."

"And it's not enough
Times are tough,
It's a wonder we all survive,
A great Oreo tragedy
On I-95, On I-95."

A job doesn't always have to be a pain in the ass.
Lifeguarding at Myrtle Beach, South Carolina.

RUNNING AWAY FROM LOVE

"Like shooting stars, we get one glimpse,
one moment in life to either partake or turn and walk away."
— from the Captain's Log

People do it all the time. Figure they'll find someone better. Look for faults in companions rather than virtues. Time usually cures this myopic immaturity. Either that, or they live lonely, incomplete lives.

Sometimes we get plain scared. My brother has lived with the same woman for 30 years. They never married. At first, it was a "sixties" thing.

Times have changed. His point of view has not.

Two grown children later, both college graduates, she would like to get married. He balks. She wants commitment.

Anita and I had been together three years. When it came to marriage, I was still uncertain, for reasons unknown.

Other gun-shy thoughts had to do with my first marriage. Divorce is tough, regardless of who initiates the process. I didn't want to go through the hurt it always seems to bring, again.

I shut down emotionally, anxious now to get back to South Florida, secure aboard my love, *Physalia*.

Not a cruel person, most of my actions were unconscious. Except for rare exceptions, I am considered sensitive and caring. Other less admirable terms of address are spitefully administered on occasion. This is life. We are all human, subject to moments of impropriety and indiscretion.

Still, we can pay dearly.

As fall approached, we moved further apart. I went back to teaching; she a student, working part-time.

Not long after I had written "The Great Oreo Tragedy," I met Bill Todd, a struggling performer and jack-of-all-trades. I needed a melody. The chorus had come to me on I-95 like a bird trill on the wind.

Sitting in my sailboat cockpit, guitars in our laps, we combined efforts, settling on a talking folk song approach that quickly became part of his repertoire.

Performing at the English Pub on Key Biscayne, New Year's Eve, my date and I entered the upstairs lounge as Bill tuned his guitar, preparing for the evening.

A group of single women at the bar started chanting in unison: "Oreo, Oreo, Oreo."

Seeing me enter, Bill told the Oreo fans that the writer had arrived and called me onstage to kick off his first set. We welcomed the New Year on the same notes.

Next time we performed was outside at Monty Trainer's. I invited Anita. It only seemed appropriate.

On a Sunday afternoon in January, at the most popular spot in Coconut Grove, we took stage along with my friend Eric, who played guitar, backed up by house performer Dink Ramsey and his band, The Calypso Angels.

Eric's girlfriend, Jenine, a sexy, raven-haired, out-of-control woman, skimpily clad, tossed Oreos on stage. Anita left when Janine jumped onstage and threw her arms around me, planting a kiss on my cheek.

I didn't see it coming. Didn't mean anything anyway. She was merely cocaine induced overly enthusiastic.

Timing is everything.

We spoke even less frequently into springtime.

A good friend, Bill Bigham, would come down to visit from South Carolina.

Bill had moved to Myrtle Beach from inland South Carolina when he was seventeen. Sand in his shoes, he became a lifeguard. My brother was also a lifeguard and Bill's roommate.

Returning to the university after my five-year hiatus as a journalist, I spent the next two summers with my wife and daughter, working as a lifeguard. I graduated, moved to Florida, and started my series of careers. I separated in 1975 and divorced in 1978.

Bill stayed on the beach, bought lifeguard franchises, and made a good living working tourists Easter through Labor Day.

Now divorced with two children of his own, Bill sat with me aboard *Physalia* at Dinner Key Marina.

He had a proposal.

He was opening a new lifeguard station at Litchfield Beach and wanted to know if I would take the position.

He knew I wasn't teaching, that Anita was not a factor in my life and wanted a friend to share summertime on the Grand Strand.

"Don't you think I'm getting a little old?" I asked, having crossed the forbidden fortieth meridian.

"You're in great physical shape. Besides, Litchfield is quiet: just upscale families. Not the garden-variety drunken tourist. You can kick back and write poetry."

"Besides," he continued, "what else are you going to do? I know you don't teach summers."

He had a point. I had been offered some boat deliveries down island, but sitting on the beach, penning succulent words of erotic passion, with the possibility of meeting a new woman, seemed more appealing.

If we turn our backs on opportunities seldom presented, they usually don't reappear.

Like shooting stars, we get one glimpse, one moment in life to either partake or turn and walk away. There aren't that many second chances, in shooting stars, love, and lifeguarding after forty.

I signed on.

Kicked back with a glass of merlot in *Physalia*'s cockpit spinning small talk with Jo Ann, dock master and sometimes social companion, only two days away from departure to the Carolina coast, the surprise came with Anita's appearance.

Here it was, late May in Miami, hot and humid, Anita carrying an armload of my old flannel shirts and winter apparel left in her apartment when we separated. "Thought you might need these," she said, stepping aboard as if invited, like we hadn't talked for weeks. She went below, making herself at home, arranging clothing in the small hanging forward locker.

"I'd better leave," Jo Ann said, obviously as equally surprised and uneasy with the situation. We had been dating some the past six months.

"Don't you dare!" I declared.

Coming back on deck just as Stan and Muriel, walking down the dock, paused to ask when I was leaving, Anita blanched at my hasty response. "Day after tomorrow," I said.

"Have a great time in South Carolina. See you in September," they said, resuming their walk.

"What are you doing in South Carolina?" Anita asked, a mix of astonishment, fear, and loathing.

"I've got to go," Jo Ann said, not accepting a possible restraint, putting down the wine glass and climbing over the lifelines onto the dock. "Talk to you later. Give me a call."

"So, what's this about South Carolina?" Anita asked again.

"Decided to do something serious with my life," I replied with more than a hint of sarcasm. "Going to be a lifeguard."

Neither said anything.

"Would you like a glass of wine?" I finally offered.

She said yes. I poured one glass, then another.

There is something to be said for intimate moments that come from the heart when least expected, like a depth charge.

This was one of those moments.

You cling, like finger nailing a cliff edge, to emotions you're convinced are true, slipping slowly into the abyss.

"We need to talk," she said. "How about dinner?"

"I already have plans," I told her.

"Then how about tomorrow? You leave the next day."

I feared the outcome, a new beginning to what had taken so long to end. Opening old wounds served no purpose.

I was moving on.

"Look," I said gently, "I'm a vagabond poet priest. I live on a sailboat. You need and deserve more than I could offer. I'm not going to work a regular job or lead a life most people do. This is who I am. A romantic and a dreamer."

She looked up with tears in her eyes.

"That's the person I fell in love with," she said, "the one I want."

We had dinner atop Coconut Grove Hotel. I wore a white linen suit and Panama hat. She a tropical shoulder-strap dress.

She stayed overnight. We made love tenderly.

The next morning, I put my surfboard on top of the VW, and loaded my bike, typewriter, books, and the teddy bear, a birth gift from my mother's sorority sister, that has been a lifelong companion.

Anita left before I locked *Physalia* and drove away.

Said she couldn't watch.

She had called several times before I arrived on the Carolina coast at Bill's home.

She called every day for six weeks, until, despite my reservations, she got in her Toyota and drove north, arriving one afternoon at my lifeguard stand unannounced.

That night we phoned her parents. Told them we were getting married.

On September 3, Labor Day, 1984, me wearing tuxedo tails and a Panama hat, she in white silk and flowered hair ornament, both barefoot, my grandmother as best man, my childhood teddy bear propped in the lifeguard chair, adorned with my son's deck shoes, we were married at sunset by the justice of the peace.

Everything you need as a lifeguard.
VW Bug, surfboard, bicycle, typewriter and teddy bear.

A few bystanders gawk as Elvis pulls into his driveway in Memphis, Tennessee.

SARAMONT ROAD AND ELVIS

"My belief is we are here for a purpose.
I keep struggling for answers."
— from the Captain's Log

I grew up in the South on a dirt road across the street from a city park. Actually, we moved to Saramont Road when I was midway through third grade, a bicycle ride away from Brennan Elementary School.

Cold weather isn't my thing.

Memories still linger of iced fingers pedaling up steep and rocky Saramont Road.

A neighborhood in the making, Dad cleared the one-acre, heavily wooded lot to build Mother's dream home: three bed-rooms with basement. Mother wanted the basement because she had storm phobia.

Toto would be amused.

Tornadoes are about as frequent as blizzards in Columbia, South Carolina. I recall a few tornadoes, never a blizzard.

A model homemaker and hypochondriac, Mother wasn't too thrilled when Dad bought a tractor and plowed the back-yard into a mini farm.

Her idea of communing with nature was a trip to the mall.

To this day, her passion is shopping.

What she wanted and eventually got, long after I had left home, was a swimming pool.

Dad loved storms. He grew up on a farm during the Depression. Storms meant rain for crops. Lightning and thunder were as good as liquid gold. He used to lie in bed with my brother Les and me, watching storms, describing their virtues as good friends bestow compliments.

Our family is weather freaky. A newsbreak on the Second Coming would take a back seat to a tropical weather update.

Growing up, I never liked Columbia.

Something I sensed as a child about rules and regulations, social taboos, provincial thinking, and racial prejudice depleted my spirit. Now I can articulate these negative emotions I felt.

Then I couldn't.

When Dad was transferred to Memphis, Tennessee, my world expanded. An executive with Havertys Furniture Company, he seized the moment to advance. So did I.

Now I knew my dislike for Columbia was not paranoia. Energy filled my body like solar flares racing across the surface of a sun.

Elvis lived within walking distance at 1034 Audubon Dr, which he bought for $40,000 in March 1956 for his parents Vernon and Gladys, as well as himself, using the royalties from his song *Heartbreak Hotel*.

He was on the verge of hitting stardom. Still living in the ranch-style house with a double carport, a few fans would stop by and gawk. To this day I am not and have never been a groupie. I simply liked Elvis' music.

Knocking on Elvis' door, the maid would politely reply to my request to see Elvis.

"Mister Elvis is not here," she might say, or,

"Mister Elvis is on the patio meeting with some gentlemen."

Without hesitation, my brother Les, almost three years my junior, and I brazenly walked into the carport, past the pink Cadillac, and white Cadillac, up to the white picket fence, and peered around the corner at Elvis, sitting on the patio in his purple silk shirt, white pants and suede shoes, and watched as he met with his businessmen.

A little old lady, or so she seemed at the time, was dusting dirt from Elvis' car into an envelope. I thought then, and still to this day, there is something strange about foolish fanfare. She proved the point indubitably.

Elvis was a cool guy. He saw us and came over to talk. A swimming pool had just been installed. Elvis turned his back when the little ol' lady, probably 30-years-old, made suggestive comments, and he pretended to take off his pants, as though he might go swimming.

Assholes are abundant. One had appeared from nowhere. Knowing Elvis didn't swim, he made an uncomplimentary comment to that effect. A moment in time was tainted.

We must be careful what we say and when we say it, and perhaps more prudent, what we think. A misplaced thought is as lethal as rat poison.

Elvis was disappointed. He didn't like rejection. Years proved this to be the case.

One day, walking to Elvis' for lack of anything else better to do during summer school recess, he pulled into the driveway with a blonde, got out of his car, came around, and like a typical Southern gentleman, trained in manners in Tupelo, Mississippi, where he was born, he opened her door.

"Hey Elvis, how about a picture with me and my brother?"

233

I asked. There were three of us, no one else, standing in the driveway: my brother Les, June, this ditsy daughter of my mother's closest friend in Memphis, and myself.

Wrapping his arms around Les and myself, June took the photos. Back then there were no doubles. You got what you got. One photo. We took a whole sequence, not only with Elvis, but of his house and lawn.

Six months after moving to Memphis, Dad got a call from Atlanta, headquarters for Haverty Furniture. Mister Dinkins, manager of the Columbia, South Carolina, stores, had died.

Cancer.

An offer was on the table. He could take over as manager of both Columbia stores, go back to his birthplace, move back into the dream home on Saramont Road, return to all lifetime alliances, and resume life as it had been.

Home free, released from limited thought processes, approaching fourteen years old, I had experienced the Pippin, a colossal wooden roller coaster; the Cotton Carnival, a decadent and impressionistic Mardi Gras of Memphis; met Elvis; ice skated, snuck into the reputed Peabody Hotel, where Les and I crashed an all-girls fan club and were practically bludgeoned by young girls when I grabbed extra eight-by-eleven glossy Eddie Fisher autograph photos.

Two boys, we were out of context. So much so that when Fisher went to sign my photo, he asked my name automatically, but didn't hear me say "Eddie" until after he had inscribed, "To my girl..." He looked up, actually embarrassed and perplexed how a male had infiltrated an all-girls gathering. Hastily scratching through his affection, he signed his name.

I have it somewhere. Maybe.

Summer in Memphis meant love. Her name was Jean Ann Morrison. We played spin the bottle behind her house near the railroad tracks. Waynoka Lane. If she reads this book, I hope she calls. Train whistles are like soft lip magic.

Once back in South Carolina, I bought a split heart necklace, sent her one half, wore the other half myself, vowing one day to return and reunite. Like yesterday, the feeling of going to the post office on Gervais Street, mailing her package with love and affection, is indescribably delicious.

As we age, those early hormonal and fresh as spring air love feelings fade. Maybe we, as collective consciousness, fear loss, much like never again seeing Jean Ann Morrison once I had fallen in love. Perhaps we are jaded one time too many, opening our heart, sharing our feelings, and being rejected.

I yearn for love and passion like I did when I met Jean Ann Morrison, always seeking the ultimate lightness of being.

Train whistles blow in my sleep. Elvis is a part of my life. He put one arm around my neck, the other around my brother Les' and struck a pose. When we got back to South Carolina, we were like war heroes. Girls swooned as they passed around the Elvis pictures like bullion. Probably a few were captured. Maybe they will return to us someday.

Les and I shared a bedroom in our rental home on Sheffield Lane, waiting for termination of the year's lease on Sararnont Road. We also shared a bed lamp and table between twin beds.

A younger brother, Roy, a postscript in the family, eleven years my junior, was in his terrible twos stage of life. He opened the sacrosanct drawer shared by Les and myself and, while we were at school, tore the Elvis photos to shreds.

I'm stilled appropriately pissed.

So is Les.

All that remains are shards of Elvis, two autographs, and a swatch of grass from Elvis' front yard.

Random acts of violence perturb. We are supposed to be civilized people. I long for it to be different. For times to change. Simple acts of love, gathering momentum, speeding through time and space, so powerful no negative force can stop them. Orgasms in universe.

Saramont Road, I am now convinced, is an energy vortex. On the surface, Saramont Road personified early television sitcoms like *Leave It to Beaver* and *My Three Sons*. Only this one short road, with several houses and its personalities, easily could be scripted for Hollywood.

Wrapped tighter than a proverbial brick, there was more energy circulating than time in warp. I babysat for Donna Drake, a cute kid across the street who took song and dance lessons before she could talk. Paying off handsomely, she became an original dancer in *The Chorus Line*.

Her mother was sexy as hell. She lounged late.

I would go across the street to visit Logan, a strange kid who turned out even stranger in adulthood. Spoiled to his pudgy core, he was one of the first kids to own a Les Paul cherry cutaway guitar. Today they are collector's items.

Mostly, I enjoyed seeing his mother in her translucent yellow nightgown. Hormones were in motion. She was my first sexual fantasy of an older woman.

Donna, last I heard, is still living in New York City. Her mail got confused with a writer friend of mine's postal box. Small world stuff. She is living somewhere around 72nd and Amsterdam. On Broadway in *Sophisticated Ladies*, probably 10 or so years ago, I visited her backstage. Still petite and precocious, she hadn't changed much with time.

Last I heard, she was looking for work.

Her brother, from what I've been told, is quirky. Story goes he had an encounter with our next-door neighbor, Pat Tomlin. Pat is a serene soul, soft-spoken and polite. He lived in the family home until he became a multi-millionaire land developer, working for his brother Don.

Growing up, Pat and Tommy, as Don was called, were casual enemies to Les and myself. They were not allowed in our "Tiger Club" or the clubhouse we had built in the woods behind our houses.

I shot a redbird once on a treetop in their yard. Dad had a rule: don't shoot bluebirds or redbirds, everything else is fair game. He grew up in the country. Shooting for food was okay. Killing for no reason was not good. Break the rules; I'd lose my Winchester-action Red Ryder BB gun.

Tommy, now a billionaire with a Rolls-Royce and a private jet, knew the rules. He was not beyond telling on me, a primary reason he was not allowed in the Tiger Club. He was in his backyard when the shot was fired. Knowing this bird was off-limits, I fired from the hip, thinking my odds slim. The redbird rolled over, clinging to the limb.

"You killed him!" Tommy shouted, loud enough for everyone in the neighborhood to hear...

"Sleeping," I told Tommy.

"Be quiet. You're going to wake him."

He was almost convinced, when rigor mortis set in, the bird plummeting with an undeniable thud on the ground.

"See, I told you so. You shot him."

I ran into the house, knowing I would be told on.

Mother was on the phone.

"I didn't mean to kill him," I pleaded.

A small dirt street in middle-class America, Saramont Road is definitely an exception to the norm. Three houses, seven kids. One goes successfully to Broadway; Her brother turns Looney tune. The two boys next door become, as the saying goes, filthy rich, building oceanfront condos and huge upscale housing projects.

My brother Les became a smuggler. A lot of South Carolina boys moved to Key West in the late sixties and early seventies. One friend, Sid Snelgrove, now owns Sloppy Joe's, probably the most famous bar in this hemisphere. My brother Les worked for a lawn service with Jimmy Buffett. They are still close friends. Buffet is godfather to my niece.

Les went from cutting grass to selling it. Many got in the business. Most got caught. Some got away. In the seventies, marijuana was the popular drug of choice on most college campuses. Bringing forty-foot sailboats full of reefer from Colombia, South America, and Jamaica began as sport.

Soon, it was big business.

What had begun as a lark now became a global enterprise. A freighter loaded with hashish from Lebanon, with an estimated street value of $7 million, was seized off Hilton Head. Les was labeled the "kingpin."

Dubbed "Operation Jackpot," the feds began the round-up, cutting deals to get to the top.

Les fled to the white-sandy beaches of Australia with his wife and two young children.

The feds followed. Les was walking down the beach, back to their villa with a loaf of bread, when the feds busted down the front door. He was tackled in the sand.

He spent 16 years in federal. A supportive friend, Buffett performed at the Tallahassee prison. One day, weeks later, Les walked out. Six months on the lamb, he was re-captured on Florida's west coast.

Susie waited. The kids went to college. He was released in 1999 and lives a basic lifestyle in the Florida Keys, bartending at a high-end restaurant and fishing the flats.

A super athlete, my younger brother Roy played basketball for a while on a college scholarship, then switched to tennis. A natural athlete, he earned his ranking and was hired as the tennis pro at Disney World. Later, he became the tennis pro for the city of Ft. Myers.

Moneymaking was always a measurement of self-worth in our home. I emphatically rejected the notion. Roy bought it. Watching Les' net worth soar, he asked to be a player.

Initially, Les refused, not wanting another family member involved, afraid Roy couldn't take the heat when the time came. Roy bullied his way in.

He got caught and spent three years in federal prison.

Like the accomplished athlete he truly is, Roy bounced back and became a successful headhunter. A single parent with two boys in college and a daughter in eighth grade at a private school, who lives mostly with him, Roy is still state

tennis champion in his division, despite knees that are coming unglued from years of activity. He gets up
every morning at 5 a.m. to walk five miles and bicycles
in the mountains.

Being the eldest child, I am most cautious.

Most of all, I didn't want to risk freedom.

The opportunity existed. I resisted.

My wife at the time was adamant that I do not get involved.

We had two children; I was in graduate school.

Like anyone else, I gravitate to the "good life."

Like Thoreau and Kerouac, I seek alternative lifestyles rooted in simplicity. I truly want to make a difference. My belief is we are here for a purpose. I keep struggling for answers. They lead me in different directions, all interrelated and interconnected.

In 1991 I left the classroom to study more, this time in the field of mind/body/spirit medicine, a holistic approach to solutions for living and dying.

Taking it a step further, I resumed my doctoral studies in 1996, graduating on Halloween, 1999. I'm one of a small handful with a doctorate in this field.

I'm trying my best to make the most of all this effort.

I saw Elvis at the Memphis airport, headed to Hollywood to discuss what would become his first film, Love Me Tender. I captured the moment with my trusty Brownie camera.

The King is born

THE NIGHT
ROCK N ROLL WAS BORN

"I was scared stiff—everyone was hollering,
and I didn't know what they were hollering at."
— Elvis Presley

July 30, 1954: 19-year-old Elvis Presley stepped onto the stage at the Overton Park Shell in Memphis, Tennessee, for his first-ever professionally paid live performance.

Some call it the first rock 'n' roll performance in history.

He sang three songs that night. And with just those three songs, a guitar, and his gyrations, he changed everything.

Two years later, June 1, 1956, Elvis returned to the Overton Park Shell for a surprise appearance with Carl Perkins, Roy Orbison and Johnny Cash.

I call it unforgettable because I was there along with 5,000 screaming teenagers.

I saw Carl Perkins and Elvis exchanging autographs.

General admission tickets were $1.

It's not often you look back and realize you stood at the crossroads of culture and history.

I didn't know it at the time, but at age thirteen I felt it, and I knew greatness when I saw it.

Years later, when my baby brother was just a toddler, he found a drawer full of photos: pictures of me and my brother with Elvis in his driveway, his arms draped around our shoulders. And like any good toddler on a mission, he tore them all to shreds.

Gone forever. But not the memory. Not the moment.

Five-day yoga cruise to the Caribbean,
where I was invited to play Elvis in the closing evening show.

244

Home sweet home from the third grade until college.

MORE ABOUT SARAMONT ROAD

"We came through a tube, gasping for air, searching for freedom."
— from the Captain's Log

The street doesn't end here. It curves around the hill to Claremont. The Leventis' lived there. Chris was my age. We were in the same class. He was the quintessential Greek god. He had everything... looks, charm, senior class presidency.

We played football in my front yard during the season. After graduation, he did University of Virginia law school, and much to my surprise, moved to New York City. If I'm not mistaken, he became a stockbroker.

Chris died at an early age. He had everything society dictates. Looks, family, income, attractive wife, secure job, and an unlimited, boundless future. Word is suicide. Papers said he choked in his sleep. I only know his death was a loss.

His cousin Pete lived up the hill from Saramont Road. Like most of us in the neighborhood, he spent afternoons in Mays Park, playing ping-pong when the weather turned sour.

Ping-pong became a serious competition.

We had a yearly tournament at Mays Park.

What I wanted more than anything was to win the gold chain and crossed paddles. Charles Cheek was a favorite. I beat him, advanced to the finals, and faced off with Pete Leventis.

Like in all games of life, there is an underdog. Pete was it. No contest. But when the game got close to the end, he broke down and cried. Two points to win. Gold chain and paddles.

Everyone consoled Pete. I consoled Pete. When we resumed play, I threw the game, obvious to everyone.

I took the long walk across the park home.

Emotions roiling, I was not certain whether I had gratuitously given to Pete because he needed so much to win, pressured as he was to succeed, or if I had caved in to peer pressure.

Tears streamed down my face.

I went to my bedroom, contemplating my decision and the shallowness of competitiveness.

Our front lawn was long and green. It had a terrace leading to the bedroom. In the midst of my deliberations, I heard Pete. He was standing outside. Holding the ping-pong necklace upraised to my window, he said, "This is yours. You won it."

"No," I said. "It's yours. The final score."

Since that moment, no trophy has meant anything. I seldom watch the Oscars. If I do, it is for fashion.

Pete gave me an incredible gift by showing up and telling the truth. I'll always respect him for his integrity.

Several years later he, like his cousin Chris, committed suicide.

Synchronicity abounds.

When my first wife—the mother of our two children—and I separated and ultimately divorced, our daughter Kimila was first to act out.

She had been a daddy's girl, as often happens.

Competition between mother and daughter for Dad's attention ran high. You could cut tension with a nail file.

This was not new territory. As an infant, Kim had nightmares. I could relate. Her mother couldn't. She slept like a zombie. Actually, I never have met a zombie, don't know where this adage originates, much less care.

But you get the message.

Sleep has never been my preoccupation. Afraid I might miss something. Restless and filled with cerebral wanderlust, I wade through nights, longing for first daylight when I can run through the mental streets I desire.

When we separated, Mom and daughter's relationship became troubled.

Kim ran away; I tracked her down on St. Augustine Beach.

She wanted to be loved. I wanted her to be loved too, by me, her mother, grandparents, friends, but not from some wayward guy of indiscriminate choice.

Our divorce had taken a heavy toll. She felt abandoned. I put her in the car and drove back to Gainesville.

Being a parent or a child is difficult in tough times. It never gets easier. We live in an imperfect world. Or perhaps we don't. If everything is in divine order, we live in a perfect world perceiving imperfection. We often think we exist in hell as a result of wrestling with emotional, physical, monetary, and relationship dilemmas.

We go through the motions, shop malls, run away to special spots, have affairs, get drunk, go to church for redemption, and die.

This is the usual sequence. It varies, but on our planet Earth, little effort is extended to making it a better place from where we originated.

We came through a tube, gasping for air, searching for freedom. And once we get here, the message comes back: we are being held captives in a world that doesn't respect or recognize freedom and breathing.

Returning her home was a temporary statement. Not enamored of my Miami lifestyle, on a sailboat as home, nor enchanted with my young girlfriend only three years older, she balked at an invitation to live with me.

A critical moment, I took her to my parents in Columbia, South Carolina. They were stable, certainly more than I, and structured. Good, solid foundation, and willing to embrace their first grandchild.

SARAMONT ROAD.

The font of security. A street of iniquity.

At the corner of Saramont and Trenholm Road, the McCuens had bought the Finchers' home. Richard was the only boy surrounded with sisters. He married my daughter Kim.

Around the corner on Trenholm Road lived Billy and Johnny Wingfield. Their mom fixed us peanut butter and jelly sandwiches. Billy is my doctor in Charleston, South Carolina. Divorced and handsome, he looks much like I remember him in our youth.

Johnny is a wild card, spending much his life in Los Angeles and Key West, he is on the road. Haven't seen him in years. Looking forward to it. Both are part of the Saramont Road connection. Heard Johnny was a good friend with Mick Jagger. Makes sense, considering the neighborhood.

My thinking is, if you have everything and give it up, it must not be enough of what really matters. We all have agendas, as was played out on Saramont Road.

I've narrowed it down. I just want a woman in my life to share dreams, passion, and spontaneous adventures in the time we have remaining. Nothing complex, not too many formal dress occasions, mostly flip-flops and sunset wine.

"Mother, mother ocean, I have heard you call."
-Jimmy Buffett, *A Pirate Looks at Forty.*

HENRY DAVID THOREAU
AND SAILBOATS

"Thoughts are more important than words."
—from the Captain's Log

Willing to confront essential facts of life head-on, Thoreau built a small wooden cabin in the woods on Walden Pond, where he lived for two years, two months, and two days. From time to time, he would have visitors or make a trip into town, primarily for supplies.

His reflections on life, and observations on nature as seasons came and went, were recorded for posterity in his book *Walden*.

Thoreau is my hero. Not only was he willing to look deep inside himself, something most people avoid like cold grits, but also, was willing to take a risk, the lifestyle change his venture required.

On the way to my first divorce, I decided to buy and live on a 34-foot sailboat. Advice comes cheap. "Why don't you start off with something small, learn to sail, and work your way up?" was the most frequent admonition.

A dream for some years, I frequented marinas on both Florida coasts, walking the docks, looking for the right fit. I haunted brokers' offices, asking questions and plowing through their listings.

Actual experience was minimal, limited to a few sailing excursions and several lessons.

Once I bartered with a salty dog in Cape Canaveral.

He had a forty-foot yawl that he wanted to charter in the Abacos with his next-door neighbor's wife, with whom he was having an affair.

With my marketing background, I designed a brochure for his business. Salty Dog took me sailing three times, then disappeared in the Florida sunset bound for the Abacos, leaving behind his own wife and a rabid next-door neighbor.

Walking the docks at Dinner Key Marina in Coconut Grove, I stopped and talked to boat owners about life on board. Knowing most 34-foot sailboats can be single-handed, and also are big enough to sail around the world, if that became an objective, my focus was in this range.

Larry Krug, a diminutive and animated owner of *J.A.P.* (*Jewish American Princess*), a 36-foot Pearson, had just the boat in mind. Practically dragging me over to Pier Three, he introduced me to *Physalia*.

She was a stately flush-deck wooden cutter-rigged sailboat, built in New England of white cedar and oak, with a Philippine mahogany interior and diesel power, and she was priced right.

An airline pilot who had purchased her from the original owners was faced with a financial dilemma. He had to sell the boat so he could take a year's sabbatical or surrender his year of freedom and keep *Physalia*. Reluctantly, he reasoned another boat could come later. He was in early mid-life crisis, uncertain if he wanted to continue flying or change careers. A year would help him decide.

At the time, I was teaching part-time at Brevard Community College in Melbourne, Florida, a four-day sail north of Miami. A lifelong friend, who knew absolutely nothing about sailing, would join me.

After one afternoon's instruction on Biscayne Bay, I signed the papers, provisioned the boat, and headed out into the Atlantic, bound for Ft. Lauderdale, first leg of the journey.

Now this may sound foolhardy, and in retrospect it was, but you learn fast. All three sails raised, *Physalia* was clipping along like poetry in motion until the sea breeze picked up. We were so heeled over that water was coming in over the rails into the cockpit.

William thought we were tipping over. I finally figured out you can either reduce sail or sheet out the boom, letting air spill from the sail, allowing the boat to right itself. The first of many lessons learned over 16 years living aboard. A few got downright hairy.

Two summers later, my traveling companion Lisa and I crossed the Gulf Stream and entered the celebrated Bermuda Triangle, known as an area where boats and planes mysteriously disappear.

Without any sophisticated equipment, not even radar for monitoring weather or a knot-speed indication, I relied on "dead reckoning" to navigate. Estimating my speed, and checking set-and-drift chart data, I plotted our way first to Bimini, then across the banks during a violent thunderstorm to Chub Cay, and on to Nassau. Out of sight of land, a compass became my biggest ally. Without it, we would be lost.

We sailed down to the beautiful Exumas, eyeballed our way through reefs into the small cays, inhabited mostly by iguanas. I started to feel cocky about my abilities.

That's when trouble occurs.

The ocean can be awesome and unpredictable. Sailing from Spanish Wells at night across the deep Tongue of the Ocean intending to enter the dangerous reef openings near Hopetown the following morning, we had no chart knowledge on set-and-drift. It is impossible to tell which way you are being dragged just eyeballing the surface.

Relying primarily on the compass, we crossed through the Devil's Backbone and, plotting our course on a pitch-black night foreboding possible storms, began our journey. Before we had raised the sails, I painfully slammed my shin into a bronze deck air vent, leaving a golf ball-sized indentation.

Lisa had a bad feeling, but we could not go back through the Devil's Backbone, a series of just-below-the-surface reefs that will rip the bottom out of a boat like construction paper.

Sitting side by side at the helm, alternating catnaps, never fully sleeping when crossing a strange area. Lisa woke me abruptly at 3 a.m.

"Land," she said, extremely panicked, pointing straight ahead. Having consumed copious amounts of medicinal Mt. Gay rum to ease my painfully injured shinbone, I was more comatose than usual under night sail.

The wind had picked up considerably earlier. Seas had increased seven to ten feet.

Best as I could, I peered into the abysmal darkness, straining to see what she saw. Knowing we shouldn't be anywhere near landfall for at least three more hours, I wrote off her fear as exhaustive hallucination.

Starting to nod off, her voice now urgent, wagging her finger over the bow, she pleaded with me to take notice. Now fully awake, I surveyed the eerie evening, scanning the horizon for anything to indicate landfall. Then I spotted the five-second blinking light, off to the right, back over my shoulder, out to sea.

Bolting down the companionway, I checked our navigational chart. Only one light possible... Hope Town. This put us downwind and inside the long coastline of deadly reefs that extended out from shore five miles. Many a Spanish galleon ended on these reefs. To this day, gold doubloons occasionally surface on these out islands.

We had made better time than expected, driven by unexpected night winds and currents not charted in this region, pushed much further to the south. Best I could determine, we had entered Taloo Cut, north of Hole in the Wall, southern end of the Abaco chain.

This was a very narrow and only reef-free sandy stretch along the shoreline. The reality of our tenuous situation was sobering. Considering sea conditions, if we hit a reef, *Physalia* would sink in minutes at most, and we would most likely die, painfully shredded on hard coral.

Now I could see land. Directly ahead, the sensation was like hurtling toward a brick wall.

Grabbing the helm, I reversed our direction, careful to steer a reciprocal course. This meant we were going back out the same way we came in. Best as I could determine, anyway, considering currents that had set our course so far south.

Being scared under such circumstances is a given. There are no safe harbors, no Burger Kings or gas stations to pull over for a breather. You are out there in pitch-blackness all alone. Each second is forever, waiting to hear the crunching noise that may end your life.

Now, on the VHF radio, I raised a voice at Hope Town Lighthouse. "Yes, Captain, you are in dire trouble. Nothing more to do than keep your heading. Stay on course until the sun is high in the sky, so you can pick your way through the reefs into Marsh Harbor. God go with you, Mon."

With the sounds of the sea rushing beneath our sailboat's bottom, Lisa and I said few words over the next two hours, mostly sitting and wading in our thoughts, some having to do with mortality.

We are never, I thought during my moments of reflection, far from death, whether at sea, on a highway, in our bed, at work, or the movies. One breath, one reef away from the end point.

For one rare instance, I thought, get me out of this and I will never sail again. As fast as the thought came, I dismissed it with a chuckle. Lisa caught it, wanting to know what was so damn funny considering our position of peril.

"Thoughts are more important than words," I told her, explaining what had crossed my mind in a moment of divine deal making.

"We aren't supposed to die now," I said with enough confidence to ease her anxiety. "Consider this a learning experience. We move to the next level of understanding now."

"I don't think I like being in school," she laughed.

"How about a cold beer?"

"Lesson learned," I said. "Here is the church key."

*Taken from the stern while anchored
in Hopetown, Bahamas.*

Running aground is a fact of life.
If someone says otherwise, they're either a liar
or never left the dock.

MARSH HARBOR
AND HOT SHOWERS

"All in harmony with nature,
we had encountered adversity and ecstasy."
— from the Captain's Log

Nine hours later, we dropped anchor in Marsh Harbor. Our mainsail was blown out, a large gash where the battens had torn through the fabric when we jibed to avoid running aground. Rowing the dinghy ashore, we decided to luxuriate in separate showers, at one buck each, charged to those anchored offshore.

Normally, we showered together.

Having sailed for two months now, we mostly bathed on deck using a sailor-friendly H_2O bag hoisted up the mast with the halyard, usually after washing in the ocean with biodegradable peppermint soap.

Accustomed to seawater temperature, I found the hot water unpalatable. As it turned out, so did Lisa.

Henry David Thoreau would have approved.

With only the basics, a sailboat built in a New England backyard of white cedar, oak, and teak, the simplest of equipment and design, all in harmony with nature, we had encountered adversity and ecstasy.

We saw whales and giant iguanas, caught fish, and swapped happy hour ice cubes from the miniature propane refrigerator for rice and vegetables, living off sea and land.

We took our time mending sails and exploring islands in the Abacos by dinghy for a laid-back week under the guidance of common sense and spiritual direction.

We had learned many lessons.

Now was the time to take a much-needed break and reflect on how close we came to this having been our last voyage.

Physalia, by the way, with its simple yet elegant construction, is considered by boaters to be a "stately woman of the sea." It is also the Latin name for the Portuguese man-of-war, a stinging, balloon-like colonial organism often mistaken for a jellyfish.

Physalia was permanently scrolled into the timeless bowsprit. If I had renamed her, though, she would have been *Walden II*.

Jon Kabat-Zinn was my mentor
for my doctoral thesis
in Mindfulness-Based Stress Reduction.

AS CHANGE IS INEVITABLE, UNCERTAINTY IS UNCOMFORTABLE

"A butterfly lives but one day. For a butterfly, this is eternity."
— from the Captain's Log

Thinking back, there are many questionable decision times of enormous proportions that make what goes around come around. Governed by self-centeredness, self-absorption, and plain ignoring what is going on around us, except within, we often miss a larger picture of what might be, can be, and will be, if we wash the dishes.

I used this as illustration, because women bring it up often. Adolescent thinking perhaps.

I was forced to wash dishes, my brother drying, or vice versa, when we were children. We both resented this duty.

I still wrestle with why I despise the task so much. Having lived alone, fully adult, I dislike it even more.

Even Buddhist-inclined, I fight the task like a fork-and-spoon enemy. Even Jon Kabat-Zinn, friend and founder of the Center for Mindfulness at the University of Massachusetts Medical Center, admits this is his nemesis.

He says he has made peace with washing dishes. Personally, listening to him tell the story, I don't buy it. I know a dishwashing hater when I hear one.

Probably multi-layered reasons, of course some Freudian, mine is mostly hands-basic. I just don't like the feeling of hands in detergent-filled water basins. A sensual and physical turnoff, I'd rather be trudging in cow dung. Not that this is a palatable image. Just bringing home a point.

Sitting on the dock in Islamorada, Florida, with my new love, Debra, discussing how special this past month has been despite all the conflagrations, she lamented having to leave, give up our five-week hiatus, where we came for me to write.

Debra is not a quiet woman. Used to social hyperbole, she goes from one social occasion back in Charleston, South Carolina, to another. Expected to be the belle of her social circle, at least in her mind, she succumbs easily to peer demand.

Knowing she desires a quieter lifestyle at age 47, we have come together. We made a pact: give me organization, I'll teach you lifestyle value. Striking a deal, each thinking we had the easier job, we learned we both got an equal challenge, as well it should be. A proverbial draw.

For the first time today, we really talked. Shared our feelings. She likes it here. More than that, she is finding out she likes solitude, which means she is learning to like herself more than ever in her life. We can't be still and quiet and not be kind in our thinking of who we are.

Like most of us human beings, she has had her unfair share of life's offerings. She has also been blessed more than most. It is the short stick and the self-doubts that haunt our longings and torment us in darkness and dreams. We are here for a short time. She knows this. I know this.

Perhaps that is why we are together.

A butterfly lives but one day. For a butterfly, this is eternity.

Today I shared with her, honestly, about a past woman in my life, things I've never admitted to anyone. Mostly, I didn't want to share those feelings with myself.

Lisa and I were lovers. She got pregnant at the same time I was getting divorced. Good friends of both of us, Maggie and Lynne, went to the women's clinic for Lisa's abortion.

To this day, I get uneasy about how I feel. Lisa probably would have liked being married and with child. No doubt, I loved her. Time was not working then in our favor.

Her frizzy hair, which I always kidded, is fond reminder. She married, had a child, and we last crossed paths on St. Croix in the U.S. Virgin Islands. Her hair was short. I didn't immediately recognize her. She was not amused.

Heard it said more than once that love is fleeting, passing like stars in night. Wish it could be as soft as a feather falling on a calm summer day, out of nowhere, the same place love originates.

Another spontaneous camping adventure.

FACING FEAR IN YOSIMITE VALLEY

"Going back to the drawing board didn't mean starting over, rather going deep inside my core to face some more essential truths."
— from the Captain's Log

Whenen the going gets tough, the tough get going. Nice thought, when sailing is smooth.

Most of us aren't programmed and prepared enough to think clearly, walk upright, or just plain function like the few who, at least in appearance, appear to skip down the street in times of trouble.

Looking in the mirror, I freaked out.

Who I saw didn't resemble the person I had come to know as myself. Stress was etched deeply into every pore.

Times were tough. In the early stages of marital separation after seventeen years mostly together, and pretty much jobless, having reduced my workload to focus on doctoral studies, l was riddled with anxiety.

Everyone who has been there knows: the foreboding, the sense of loss, helplessness, frustration, suppressed anger, and a gamut of unidentifiable, tumultuous emotions.

My studies in mind/body/spirit medicine and transpersonal psychology made the situation even more charged. Supposedly, I knew the answers, so I should invoke the solution.

What I learned is that you can often do for others what you can't do for yourself.

The optimal wellness package I had put together for individuals to take to their personal bank of stress was coming undone at the seams.

Going back to the drawing board didn't mean starting over, rather going deep inside my core to face some more essential truths.

School, I was coming to quickly realize, was not out for summer, like it had been in grade school. I had created my own box. Now forced to look elsewhere, I discovered myself doing what I was asking others to be wary of.

The research out there is somewhat limited. Medicine, even alternative and complementary healing modalities, tries to seamlessly package their stuff.

Optimal wellness was more than meditation, body scanning, exercise, tai chi, and nutrition. I needed to face some long-term, suppressed demons head-on.

If we listen to our gut, we get answers. Usually what we think we hear initially is what we truly desire.

I practice this theory in the grocery, touring aisles until some item pulls me to it. My body is communicating what enzymes and building materials are most needed.

For this reason, I shop every day, paying attention to my body's innate intelligence, eavesdropping on communication between body and mind. If I leave it alone, it serves me well. My ego remains outside, nervously pacing, if metaphorically we can accept ego as separate from that which we really want so much to be in control.

Looking in the mirror that stressful day, I took action, calling my friend Paul Canali in Miami, a holistic chiropractic physician.

At first chatty, then sharing my consternation, he suggested joining him for a journey to San Jose, California,
to attend a "transformational gate": an intense several days
of spinal adjustments, formal and informal meditation prac-
tices, and other activities designed to "clear out" the
central nervous system.

It sounded like what I most needed.

Afterwards, we would hike a week in Yosemite National
Park, climbing waterfalls and bathing in frigid mountain
streams. It would clean out tension, he assured.

Just two months earlier, I had voluntarily "bumped" a returning conference flight and spent two hours extra in
Atlanta's airport in exchange for a round-trip ticket anywhere
in the States.

Five minutes later I called Paul back.

"Meet you in San Jose," I said.

Wrapped tighter than a proverbial drum, three days de-
compressing helped.

Driving to Yosemite along the Merced River, Paul pulled
the rental off to the shoulder.

"No time like the present," he said, climbing down the
rocky ledge, pulling off his shirt and plunging into the frigid
California waters.

I stuck my foot in and retracted it just as quickly. "No
way," I said. "Too damn cold." Paul had swum to the other side.

"You've got to do it," he insisted.

"This is what you came for."

I had other ideas on this theme. Not a cold-water person, I
prefer summer warmed tropical 85-degree temperatures.

What the hell, I thought, remembering my self-portrait before making the trip. If my memory served me accurate, frostbite might be an improvement.

Literally and figuratively, I took the plunge.

Swimming briskly to the sun-warmed rocks on the opposite side where Paul lay basking, I recalled sailing solo once from Daytona Beach to Titusville, Florida.

On the last leg of my journey, I got caught in a vicious summer squall. A whiteout, unable to fully open my eyes against the stinging hurricane force driven rains, I managed to set the anchor securely.

A narrow channel on a large body of water, I could only hope no other boats would be foolhardy enough to continue underway, running such a high risk of hitting another boat or channel marker.

The storm lasted an hour. When it let up, the sky cleared as if nothing had happened, the water glassy and peaceful.

Lisa was waiting anxiously at the marina when I pulled up to the dock, my foot steering the wooden helm, more confident than I had ever been on the boat. I had looked into the eye of adversity and prevailed. The experience made me a better, more confident person and seaman.

Turned out the storm was the worst in an hour's duration on records in Titusville's history.

Leaping into icy mountain waters isn't quite the equivalent, but I experienced a prelude of what was to come the next day as we hiked up the narrow trail toward Yosemite Falls.

Every nerve in my mind and body was still tuned as tight as a piano string. Lightweight hikers were left in the dust. We were alone on the trail as it became narrower with each twist and turn.

Not fond of heights, and already emotionally challenged, I balked as we rounded the next turn, looking down the drop-off way, way, down into the valley below.

I was stuck! Insides and outside. "Something I haven't told you before," I said, calling to Paul who had disappeared around the curve. "I can't do heights. Not now, anyway."

I knew what he was going to say before he said it. Same speech I had heard the day before. Falling off cliffs is different than swimming icy streams, though.

"Grab my wrist," he urged.

"You can do it. This is why you're here."

Once again, I recalled my years earlier sailing adventure. At one point in the storm, I thought, "It can't get any worse than this. I'm in a whiteout."

Turns out I wasn't in a whiteout, not then, not at that moment I thought the thought. The whiteout came a few minutes later, almost as though I had asked for it.

"Damn I hate these tests that involve living on the edge, this close to death," I thought, grabbing his wrist, my back pressed tightly against the ledge. And yet here I am again, only this time on a mountain instead of the sea.

A ways further the path widened. We came to a small clearing with one scraggly tree growing in a safe spot. Paul walked to the edge, urging me to join him.

Having gone this far, yet still hesitant, I slowly inched my way, looking out over the valley that appeared miniature at this elevation.

"Scream!" he said. "Let it go."

Bloodcurdling would have been a gross understatement. If anyone had been following, I'm certain they would have been backpedaling at record pace once I had let go.

Feeling the tension release, I finally backed to the tree, tears rolling down my face. Sitting on the ground, a blue bird landed just inches from where I was sweating profusely. Chattering as though lecturing me, both Paul and I were transfixed.

Here we were, perched on this ledge, having what amounted to a surreal sermon from a bird. An omen.

Omens are just that. Which is why they are called omens.

We had just experienced an omen.

Climbing still higher, the trees and pathway ended, leaving us to climb over rocks, marking our trail so we could find our way back, moving closer toward the gigantic Yosemite Falls.

Tons of water pounded the hard rock, then cascaded downward to the next level hundreds of feet below, carrying boulders in its pathway, thundering like strike sounds in a giant bowling alley.

This was a dangerous excursion and Paul wanted to push it to the limit.

Yosemite Falls, at 2,425 feet, is the tallest waterfall in North America. Warning signs urge hikers not to stray from the marked path. It's a long way down from the trail of no return, and once you leave it, the path is not easy to find again.

Paul's idea was to cross the slick rocks and lounge in the pool at the base of the falls, looking up at the rainbows in one of the most scenic places imaginable. We climbed over boulders, marking the trail back with stones. The objective: to get as close to the bottom of the magnificent falls as possible.

Despite my propensity for going where others fear to tread, this was not on my bucket list.

Relegated to reality, we stretched out on the dry rock, soaked up the Chi, ate lunch, and hiked back down the mountainside.

The climb back to the base of Yosemite Falls was the most difficult hike I ever attempted. The excursion took the entire day and left me suffering from shin splints for the next three.

Back at Yosemite Mountain Lodge, we invited Susan, a schoolteacher and front desk clerk during the summer season, to join us for dinner, our treat. She had done us a big favor upon arrival, finding a cabin during high season when there were supposedly no vacancies.

As we shared our day's adventures, her face went pale and her eyes said it all.

"You two must be crazy," she sputtered. "Last week, two visitors slid off that same rock and fell to their death."

After dinner and goodnights, Paul and I drove to a nearby store, bought a jar of honey, and headed to the edge of the forest next to the parking lot. We slathered the honey on a fallen tree and sat in the car a short distance away, waiting for a bear sighting.

None showed up.

But after a day like that, it was time for bed.

It's a bird! It's a plane!
No, it's Captain Madness on his 50th birthday.

THE GOOD AND SIMPLE
AND HARD LIFE

"Our best comes from heart."
— *from the Captain's Log*

I live a good life. By sane standards, it stays simple, yet complex in its adventure qualities. Living on the edge, I don't mind taking risks, whether in romance, work choices, or pure unadulterated fun.

Some things I do one time only, at least for now, like free-falling 13, 000 feet on my birthday to test my longevity.

No loved ones watching, it was my decision alone.

I may do it again.

Doesn't really matter.

I jumped.

Stretched my left leg out on the strut.

Pulled myself out and fell backwards into space.

And eternity.

From Juno Beach, I had driven to Cape Canaveral to watch a shuttle launch. My wife was working. She couldn't take time off. In retrospect, we were winding down, too.

A spur-of-the-moment episode in one's life, which I heartily endorse, thinking perhaps these are our best moments, unplanned with unpredictable results. I drove south on A1A to a small airport outpost at Sebastian Inlet.

Difficult to find, it is stranger to imagine.

Inside the terminal, if you had a leisurely enough mind to describe it as such, a gang of offbeat degenerate-looking guys with beards and bandanas and one slightly cute, but equally and obviously independent woman, were kicking hacky sacs around the room, mostly empty except for a cola machine.

I really mean empty and lonely.

An outpost in Florida's outback.

Nothing outside except one small, single-engine derelict plane, a strip of tarmac the size of a suburban driveway and miles of weed grass.

I had phoned earlier. In fact, I had phoned all along my I-95 pathway to Cape Canaveral, where I had a press gate pass courtesy of Ron Lindsey, a photographer at Cocoa Today, the newspaper where I once wrote Sunday supplement articles, some fabricated, others true.

I always requested Ron on assignment. A laid-back guy, Lindsey kept a lid of quality reefer in his camera bag. Our trips together were kaleidoscopic.

What I yearned to do, though, was jump out of a plane at high noon as the rocket soared skyward. Polarities in motion.

Things didn't work out. Couldn't connect on phones. This was not a sophisticated kind of outfit.

Instead, I jumped after the launch at sunset. Totally sober yet soaked in adrenaline. For three days afterward, the physical experience lingered.

I'd recommend it for everyone on planet EARTH.

I have a theory. Think Thoreau would agree.

The more we need to be something other than what we feel deep inside, that inner voice calling to us saying its prayers and doing prostrations on our essence, the farther removed we are from living.

How easy to become clones of society, following contemporary templates, led like Hitler's angels and lemmings to cliff sides.

Offensive I write this, challenging righteous indignation, making such comparisons, Hitler and lemmings, sheep led to slaughter. We all must make our own bed, decide for self, not listening to others, which way we want to go.

How do you want to soar? Listening to a Nation of Lawyers? Waiting for something else to happen to make you happier than you yourself know in your heart is true?

Take a risk. Bungee jump.

If this doesn't work, ask the man or woman you love to do something out of context, kinky, risky. Make love in public. Run naked down to the beach on a full moon. Live with someone you should not for legal reasons.

But for God's sake, don't stagnate.

Don't sit for years in some antiquated belief system that becomes dung of the highest disdain.

We are creatures of God. Therefore, we are protected. All our decisions are God-related. Coming from good intention and right action, we are always rewarded.

Our best comes from heart. We must journey inside and understand that we, as individuals and collective consciousness even, we are exactly where we need to be in this space and time.

I have a girlfriend. We are lovers, sharing secrets and fantasies and spaces of the heart.

We both are generous in different ways.

She is having a difficult time in her life. As she endures, I move closer to her, actually loving her more for her willingness to admit vulnerability.

She is more human, more alive. Being vulnerable is not an affectation, not a weakness. It is being.

Like most of us earthy creatures, we want to hug in darkness and moonlight, knowing we are cared for,
on equal terms.

My girlfriend, my best friend, my lover; we are learning how this really works when times are strained, when night winds of winters in our souls howl.

She is soaked in sweat of her own dilemma, hoping for answers yet unknown.

I will tango with her in this abyss until we both unravel, and life as we are accustomed, resumes its course.

"Blue Moon," in Cracker Boy Boatyard, Riviera Beach, Florida, undergoing a ridiculous million-dollar renovation.

LOOKING FOR OPTIONS
Blue Moon

"Get on the boat. Trust the ride."
— from the Captain's Log

Maybe it has to do with my astrological sign. Scorpios are reputed wanderers and womanizers. The combination fits.

More than likely, my restlessness has more to do with purpose. Let's just say that I'm not driving the ship. In a metaphysical sense, this means all things done and said in life are for a higher purpose.

If, for example, I hadn't been repulsed by retail, I wouldn't have pursued radio, which led to journalism, and then to marketing, and back to graduate school, teaching in colleges and universities, marrying a student, more graduate studies in an emerging field of energy and consciousness, and all these experiences, and those tantamount to those experiences, are grist for the mill of this book coming home to roost.

As I reflect on past circumstances, one funneling into another, there were too many acts of synchronicity to be dismissed as mere coincidence. Like building blocks, each action has caused reaction.

Take my decision to live a Thoreau-style life on a sailboat. And consider that I "just happened" to be offered a position as humanities director at Bethune-Cookman College in Daytona Beach.

At this precise moment in time, the assistant dock master decided to commute nightly for two weeks to Jacksonville Beach for a Captain's license study course.

He wanted company. I went along for the ride. We both received 100-ton Master's licenses. Mine has served me well. After moving to Miami, I ran charters back and forth to the Bahamas during spring break. Setting up my own part-time company, I organized high-end, all-day catered charters in Coconut Grove for celebrities.

Later, fed up with academic bureaucracy, my captain's license got my wife and me a team job on a sixty-foot schooner in lovely Tortola, British Virgin Islands, for a year. With my credentials, I served as captain; she was the gourmet cook and first mate.

Never knowing what life may present along the path, I maintain my captain's credentials, renewing every five years. Starting over from scratch would be hell.

So it came as no surprise when I received a call from one of my best friends since childhood. Managing partner in a large successful law firm in Charleston, S.C., Neil Robinson was considering buying a yacht: a vintage 68-foot all wooden Trumpy, hull number 409. He asked if I would meet him in Ft. Lauderdale and give him my opinion.

Neil had never owned a boat. Not even a skiff. Appreciative of the aesthetics, he had a keen eye for beauty. A boat with history and integrity, she looked especially regal among the sleek fiberglass neighborhood afloat.

Having owned a wooden sailboat for 11 years, my advice to my novice friend was simple: Buy a fiberglass boat.

My reasons were practical.

Wooden boats require constant maintenance. All boats do, but you can get away with a lot more with plastic.

Secondly, varnish work would require constant, constant attention. Start at the bow, work to the stern, and then start over again.

"But you're the poet," he protested,

"and you owned a wooden boat you loved."

What Neil had really asked for was validation.

"That is precisely why I am offering this advice," I countered.

"I need a boondoggle," Neil joked, saying he had once owned a restaurant, then a bar, and both went belly up.

"Then you're making the right decision buying a yacht," I agreed. No doubt about it, *Blue Moon,* as he later renamed her, got my fancy. With the walnut interior and the commodious fantail for entertaining, she was definitely a dowager, stately old lady of the sea.

Trumpys were traditionally designed to order from magnates like DuPont, Firestone, and the Howard Hugheses of the world. A Trumpy book lists all present and past owners.

Trumpy, a perfectionist and eccentric, quit building boats in 1974. Not wishing to chance a lesser-quality yacht with his name, he refused to let his son continue the firm. There are about fifty left in the world.

A captain and first mate, employed on the boat for five years, were eager to stay aboard as crew, giving Neil a false comfort level.

My primary words of caution, once it was apparent Neil was intent on purchasing the boat, as he discussed the proposal in terms of endearment over coffee later that evening sitting at an outdoor cafe on Las Olas Boulevard, were to have it thoroughly surveyed. I would be glad to locate a wooden boat expert in Miami.

Saying he had it under control, the papers were drawn in November 1998.

The phone call came from Neil the next May. Living in Juno Beach, Florida, in my one-bedroom condo, putting finishing touches on my doctoral thesis for the final committee meeting, he asked if I could check on *Blue Moon*.

Seems the captain had resigned, along with the first mate. The yacht had been dry-docked for repairs in January, somewhere, he believed, close to my residence.

The boat's delivery had been promised for May, so he could motor to Annapolis, Maryland, home of the Trumpys, for an owners' first reunion.

Only six miles south, in a familiar boatyard where I used to haul out annually before I sold my second sailboat, *Raconteur,* shortly before the divorce, I drove over immediately after we hung up our conversation.

Worse than I could have imagined, she was, for all practical purposes, abandoned, planking pulled at random, leaving gaping holes in her sides.

The sister ribbing made no sense. Boats have ribs like people. When they break on boats, they are replaced, or supporting strips of wood, called sister ribs, are attached. What I saw was a butcher job. *Blue Moon* would definitely not make her reunion.

With great reservation, I phoned my buddy back in Charleston, relaying the grim news. Devastated, he asked if I could take over, at least temporarily, until he could leave the office in three weeks. He would sign over power of attorney.

Serendipity is a funny commodity.

When you least expect it, another shift takes place.

Worn out from too much left-brain activity, my doctoral research finished, I could relegate my time and energy to Neil's boat project. Being in the outdoors might be a welcome change.

As fortune would have it, a wooden boat restorer was finishing another project in the same boatyard. He had already restored six Trumpy yachts.

Little did any of us know the project would take a year and cost one million dollars. Armed with captain credentials, I was legally qualified to deliver *Blue Moon* to Charleston.

Plans were to oversee the final interior work phase up there. Maybe I would even stay aboard, and write, or just be the captain. I had no desire to live in Charleston, even though I visited several times a year to see my daughter and her family. Those occasions, as with most family visits, were pretty much limited to her house and a walk on the beach.

Although raised in South Carolina, time allotted to Charleston was brief until my voyage on *Blue Moon*, and subsequent days, rapidly adding up. I had judgmentally put Charleston in the same category of provincial attitudes and prejudicial thinking that I had come to identify in my adolescence.

Times change. People can too. Although usually slow and resistant, we adapt if we are open in our thinking.

Lots of new thinkers had moved to Charleston, particularly during the past five years. No longer just "good old boys," although the network is still very much alive and thriving, new talent and open-mindedness have a foothold.

More than that, after more than 30 years in Florida, I rediscovered my roots and related to this thing called "Southern hospitality." Seemed everyone was friendly. Couldn't pass someone within 10 feet without an extended and warm greeting. Given a cue for conversation, they will stop and tell you their life story, getting yours in the process.

I liked the warmth, the lack of game playing, of being able to carry on conversations with women without an agenda.

When we talk serendipity now, I'm talking serious serendipity. Every time I had the mere thought of leaving, heading back to south Florida, I would have a positive encounter.

Once, twice, three times maybe, we write it off as coincidence. Not the case. Being admittedly hardheaded and stubborn, which can be positive traits, also to a fault, depending on circumstances, there comes a point when you KNOW something else is guiding.

As I've said before, YOU are not driving the boat. Someone, or something else, has the controls.

EVERY TIME I had the thought to leave, there would be a magic moment, another person usually, and maybe nature in bliss, but always something that made me stay.

The boat had dropped me off in Charleston. I wasn't supposed to be Captain. I was supposed to be in Charleston, a one-way passage to destiny.

When we get messages, and they keep coming, one layered on another, not to leave a certain place; unless we are stupid, not just belligerent or even admittedly stubborn, then we acquiesce. We go with the flow. The Tao. Like leaves in eddies waltzing around boulders in streams of our life, we too must learn how to yield, to move downstream to oceans to dreams to places outside our structured lives.

Think of life as options. You can join the rank and file. Become a car czar or a soldier of fortune. Move to Mexico where the peso is golden. Live on the beach, watching waves rolling in.

Buy a house in suburbia. Clubhouse and neighborhood parties, porch walks with candlelit brown bags, more holiday decorations than law should allow, kids everywhere in golf carts and skateboards, barbecue grills and birthday parties.

Buy a condo, a house, live in a commune, sailboat, and a cardboard box under an interstate.

Options for lifestyle. The option to be fully present in every moment. Some people fill every waking moment in activity, always "doing" to avoid "being" fully aware.

We are human beings, not human doings. We never know where fate will eventually put us, although it is certain one-day we all wind up in a box... literally.

Perhaps life's secret is to stay out of the box, the metaphorical box, for as long as possible. Show up, pay attention, tell the truth, and don't become attached to outcomes.

Get on the boat. Trust the ride.

If we let go, we will arrive where we need to be.

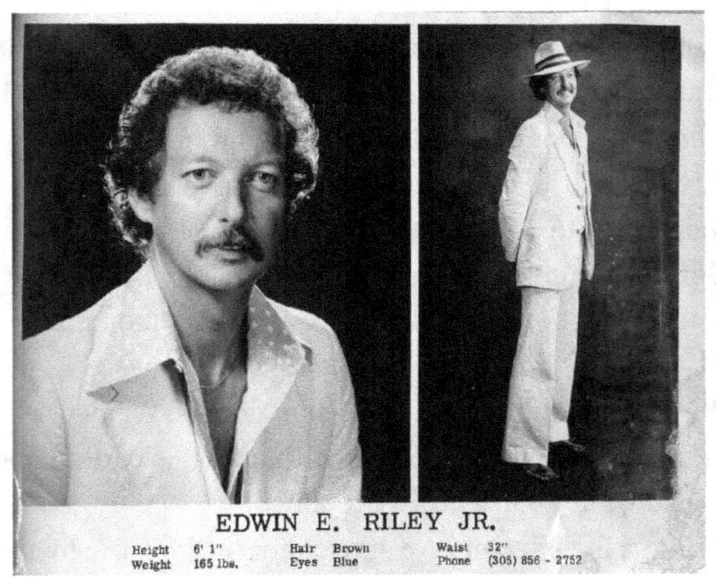

EDWIN E. RILEY JR.

Height	6' 1"	Hair	Brown	Waist	32"
Weight	165 lbs.	Eyes	Blue	Phone	(305) 856 - 2752

It was a short career, but I dug the look.
Bait for the modeling agencies.

HOW NOT TO BE AN ACTOR

"The universe is my stage. My lines are original."
— from the Captain's Log

Becoming an actor is difficult when you can't remember your lines. My first attempt came taking an acting class at the University of South Carolina back in the 1960's. Reading script was not my thing.

I like to improvise... about most everything in life. Which is why my childhood dream to become a singer didn't gel since I couldn't remember lyrics.

Being a spontaneous person, my propensity is to "feel" rather than "memorize."

Hell, I can't remember lyrics to songs I've written, requiring a prompter when I occasionally perform. Technology has changed to accommodate performers, but I grew up in an age of telephone booths and landline phones; smoking touted as being healthy allowed on airplanes.

The "not remember" list is long. (Still can't recall my last name... just kidding.)

Fast forward to 1973.

After about seven years as a journalist with Knight Ridder and Gannett newspapers, my final significant assignment covering the Apollo missions, I tendered my resignation and resumed a seemingly never-ending "professional student" education at the University of Florida.

While in Cocoa, Florida, writing special human interest features for their Sunday supplement magazine *Sunrise,* I befriended local prolific writer Martin Caidin, best known for his book *Cyborg* that was turned into the popular *Six Million Dollar Man* tv series starring Lee Majors. He also wrote the script for the popular science fiction movie *Marooned*, based on another of his books.

Then one lackadaisical day while lounging at home in the woods outside Micanopy with my St. Bernard "Elderberry" pretending to study, I get a call from Martin. "Been reading your stuff," he said. "And I'm making a movie for the annual Space Congress Convention being shown at Wolfie's ballroom on Cocoa Beach. Want you to come help."

"When?" I asked.

"Now... today," he replied.

I explained that I was 171 miles away.

"Good," he said. "You can be here for dinner."

Martin didn't take "no" for an answer. I quickly phoned my wife at work, packed a toothbrush, typewriter, surfboard atop my VW van, and drove to Cocoa Beach.

Over dinner I read Martin's screenplay. At best, it was goofy, perverse, and generally disgusting.

I was cast as Lord Sauerbraten, who would challenge the world's farting champion on a makeshift fighter's ring, loaned for the occasion, early Sunday morning in a strip club on A1A in Cocoa Beach, the audience a hodgepodge of alcoholics, derelicts and Martin's curious friends, primarily social outcasts.

My costume was a pair of his wife's pink tights with a hole cut out of the rump, aptly called the "zephyr window." I would arrive astride a bicycle built for two adorned with a wig touting a pink cigarette holder matching the tights.

Inside the fighting ring was a stripper's dancing pole. Martin played ringside announcer. I would grasp the pole alternating inappropriate sound effects with the reigning world's "farting champion."

On banquet night, the lights went down before a curious audience including a host of astronauts and local luminaries. Even Wernher von Braun was invited from Germany but thankfully declined due to illness.

Let me cut to the chase: our sense of humor was not well received. Jeers and catcalls. Finally, management shut down the projector and turned on auditorium lights as people vacated their dinner tables in a mass exit. You would have thought someone cried "FIRE." This did not compete with the movie *Titanic*... although it sunk faster.

My next "how not to be an actor" was three episodes of the popular tv series *Miami Vice*. I got the "movie extra" role coincidentally, living on a sailboat at Pier 3 in Dinner Key Marina in Coconut Grove, next to a movie site locator for Moby Marine.

In actuality, my 34-foot sailboat, *Physalia* was more the starlet. Together, we were background for filming in downtown Miami Marina. $100 for a 12–14-hour day's work sitting in *Physalia*'s cockpit drinking Heinekens. Just as well. I had no lines to learn.

However, I did have the pleasure to hang out on the film set and engage in occasional conversations with actor Don Johnson, watching the real honest-to-God alligator Elvis scare the shit out of most everyone in close contact.

Don kept his distance while making frequent references to Elvis as "that fucking dangerous reptile." I found his paranoia amusing, but then again, I was safely ensconced in my boat cockpit armed with a beer cooler and my marijuana stash.

My next foray into the cinema world was February 1991, in Charleston, S.C., as a body double, whose name I can't remember, again with no speaking lines. But I did drive a Cadillac convertible with reckless abandon in one filmed scene.

Called "Leopold Blum," it starred Dennis Hopper, Sam Shepard, and Elizabeth Shue. I got to spend time talking to each in between breaks.

Not much a theater-going fan, because I prefer doing rather than watching, I did engage in a very flirtatious conversation with Elizabeth between takes, loudly inviting to escort her around Charleston, to the dismay and disbelief of the staff onlookers who honored her demand for privacy.

But then again, how was I to know? She was sexy and friendly. They called her back to the set, and we never toured the beaches, although I must admit it was a brutally cold February. Unfortunately, so was the movie, despite such a luminous cast, and it went straight to video.

Never one to give up on a movie opportunity or red-carpet potential, I had another "almost" Welcome to Hollywood experience, cast as an extra being filmed in Miami.

Based on the Iran Contra debacle, starring Ben Affleck and Anne Hathaway, I was appropriately cast as a journalist.

My talent consisted of having wardrobe dress me in a suit with socks and pretend to take notes in a press conference sitting at a table with other pretend journalists.

Boring to the point of exertion, I turned in my wardrobe and didn't return for the next day's filming.

I made a few other half-hearted attempts as wannabe actor, primarily as an excuse to avoid what most worker bees call "a real job."

My inability to stick with a prescribed script got in the way. Too unnatural and inauthentic. I would always go off script on a tangent to express a more meaningful dialogue, one prefaced on seeking meaning and truth and virtue and compassion and spiritual evolution.

Not to sell myself short, I accomplished these lofty goals as a college professor challenging students to follow their dreams, coming from the heart rather than the status quo. Same during my stint as a journalist and psychotherapist.

What I really taught is based on tapping into one's frequency and vibration, learning how to listen to oneself and others non-judgmentally.

Now that's some sacred shit.

Raising one's consciousness.

Giving without expectation of return.

Becoming a holy person in the truest sense.

Acting? I was called to be a pirate in a film and told that I was too "pretty," had all my teeth and no facial scars.

Guess what I am is a rebel "with a cause." I still receive accolades from students who testify that my out-of-the-box teaching changed their lives, of what would most assuredly have become one of quiet desperation.

Like taking them out of the classroom, regardless the course subject, and teaching them meditation sitting on the campus lawn.

I'm a hippie and an anachronism. The universe is my stage. My lines are original. I'm constantly adapting to different roles that life presents. Guess I'm an actor after all!

Spontaneous dance on a cobblestone street in Mexico.
Sharing the vibe.

PUERTO ESCONDIDO

"We must be grounded.
If the plug to a light is not fully pushed into its socket,
the light flickers. So do we."
—from the Captain's Log

A nail-biting, prayer-filled thirty-minute flight west of Oaxaca, Mexico, lies Puerto Escondido. Down south, close to Guatemala, few Americans visit this rustic Pacific coastal village.

Most non-locals are European or Canadian. Surfers come from everywhere to ride powerful waves along a stretch of beach unsafe to swim.

Rural and undeveloped, at the base of a mountain range that drops down to the sea, you will not find condominiums and upscale boutiques.

Puerto Escondido is refreshing, a haven for expatriates and adventurers. Nudity is not uncommon on the wide, soft white-sand beach. Few rules exist.

Surfer Beach bends around an outcropping of rocks to a more passive bay where Mexican fishermen launch their boats pulled up on shore.

The water is warm and clean. Coconut palms fringe the shoreline lined with informal, open-air palapa bars, small restaurants, and bungalows.

Just back off the beach, local artisans sell handcrafted clothing and woodwork from tiny makeshift cubicles. No one speaks English. Everyone is friendly.

My muse TOOK me to Puerto Escondido. Not so much what I had read or been told, just a feeling of desiring to go that compelled my trip from Oaxaca back over the mountains.

You can get there by car. It takes seven hours if the roads are passable. Rugged terrain, often laced with banditos; you take your chances.

Hermila Gonzalez is the grand dame curandero in Oaxaca. A traditional healer, she diagnoses illness and disease by rubbing two eggs up and down the patient. Breaking the eggs into a water-filled mason jar, she then does a reading.

She claims the embryos entrain with human cells. People come from miles for her treatments. Her back room is filled with roots and herbs. She mixes and matches the formulas, blending them into a tea.

During the treatment, she "pulls" disease from patients, taking mouthfuls of mescal and spewing it across the floor to avoid infection retention. At lunch, she covets two beers and mescal chasers. A personal daily ritual.

This was my second time to study with Hermila.

Puerto Escondido was a side trip.

Small planes in the outback are unpredictable. So are the routes. Detours can be the norm.

Most secondhand planes lack ventilation. Pilots and passengers sweat profusely.

A whining, grating engine noise put us all on edge.

"Don't worry," joked one passenger, "We're all going to die of suffocation before we hit the mountain."

Getting to Puerto Escondido and back can be disconcerting, but few planes crash, at least that's what I was told. No one wishes to elaborate.

Once over the mountains, the descent is quick. Puerto Escondido lies practically at the mountain's base. Still in its natural state, the coconut palm and banana tree studded countryside runs down the mountains to the shoreline.

When life becomes noticeably unpleasant, our bodies need nurturing. This is a basic biological and neural need.

I've found the best healing comes from immersing myself in nature. We must be grounded. If the plug to a light is not fully pushed into its socket, the light flickers. So do we.

A notice was posted on the Santa Fe Hotel's bulletin board. Up the hill overlooking Surfer Beach was a holistic center offering massages and sweat lodges.

Rains gut roads in countries where they lack minimum infrastructure. Trying to walk up the washed-out clay would be like climbing a stick of butter. A bumpy cab ride did the trick.

A cultural anthropologist who had dropped out married an Indian meditator. They set up shop on this hillside, building a modest office with living accommodations. There was a large ceremonial sweat lodge and two mini-sweat lodges with redwood seats to accommodate one or two persons.

Ambitious yet basic, the center had an outdoor mosaic meditation area and two bamboo air-cooled rooms for massage that led down the stone pathway.

The massage came first. As Pamela put sheets on the massage table, she told me to undress.

In the United States, most therapists leave the room.

We are told to pull a sheet over us.

Pamela had no intention of leaving the room. There was no top sheet or covering of any kind. I stripped and climbed onto the table. She climbed on the table several times to leverage her hands for optimal range of motion.

For ninety minutes, I was rubbed and manipulated, then given a towel for the walk down to the sweat lodge. A young Mexican man had heated the volcanic coals inside the lodge. A bowl was filled with water and herbs to stoke the fire and lungs for cleansing. He would shovel more coals from the outside in fifteen minutes to keep heat going.

No longer than forty-five minutes, I was instructed, then come up the hill to the outdoor showers. A green herbal drink would be waiting on the table.

I met a couple from Montreal. They had done the sweat lodge. Every year they come in January and stay longer. Plans called for three months next year.

Pamela's husband would take us back to our places. Relaxed beyond my wildest expectations, the cost for all services was $20.

In February 2000, this was unheard of. I quickly computed. Three treatments weekly for a month comes to $240. My "Don Quixote" oceanfront bungalow was $24 nightly. Breakfast at the outdoor cafe, fresh papaya juice, and real yogurt over granola and fruit, two dollars. Sitting poolside, candlelit table, lobster and tuna platter, seven dollars.

I could live like a king on $1,200 a month. This thought still lingers. Usually, special experiences are never the same. They become inflated. Others only get better in time.

As the Pacific sun was setting, I walked across to the beach. Only a few folks remained, some sitting down by the water, waiting for the day to transition to night.

One primary way I ground myself is through tai chi, a 108-movement form usually taking twenty minutes. As I faced the Pacific and began my slow movements, I heard a flute coming from somewhere behind me.

I turned, and there, sitting in the sand with her rottweiler puppy, was a young woman in her early twenties. She smiled. I smiled back, turned and began my practice.

She played to my every movement. If I paused, the music shifted. Like being in a movie, several bareback horse riders galloped through the setting sun.

Finishing the tai chi form, I turned and bowed, then sat in the sand, all pastel blues and pinks from the setting sun filling the horizon. Closing my eyes, I felt a presence.

The young woman was sitting a foot away in the sand, facing me, her dog at her feet. She spoke some English. I speak some Spanish. We had no difficulty conversing.

Of Mexican descent, she was too on a life journey, uncertain where she would next go, or when. Here, in Puerto Escondido, she had a job at night shaping boogie boards.

We talked well into darkness. She had to work.

I walked her to her scooter parked in the sand at the pathway. Her pup climbed aboard, too large to fit end to end, hanging over both sides.

She asked when I would return. "November, at the earliest," I replied. No guarantees she would be there.

She would look for me.

Like two lovers in movies no longer made, we held each other, kissed on the cheek, and she drove away, looking back once, a smile on her face.

Two summers ago, from the time I am writing this in 2002, I arrived in Charleston. For six months, my thoughts were of moving to Puerto Escondido at least January through March.

My greatest obstacle was myself. Social conditioning rooted in fear doesn't lend itself to pursuing dreams of the heart and basic instincts.

I'm better at pushing social obstacles aside than most. The eldest of three boys, roots of responsibility grow deep. Old stories and tapes keep replaying, like a phonograph gone mad.

I know the passion of standing on a lonesome highway 3,000 miles from home, my thumb as best friend, calling for a stranger to move us to the next destination.

And I know pure love on a sandy beach at sunset in southern Mexico with a stranger who plays the flute as I dance to the gods of magic.

Fishing boats in the harbor, Puerto Escondito, Mexico.

Sometimes you win, sometimes you lose,
but what matters most is to keep on smiling.

LIFE IS HIGHLY UNPREDICTABLE AND ALWAYS UNCERTAIN

"Love is the only way through abysmal challenges.
Goodness will prevail as long as we don't get attached
to the outcome."
— from the Captain's Log

Just when we figure it out, think we have it made, life does a cartwheel. Put more succinctly, a belly flop, putting us back at square root one.

Take my significant other, my girlfriend, my delightful companion. Last week, lovers. This week, a stalemate.

We've hit a wall.

My female companion, lover, and friend is stressed out. She has good reason. Her financial security is at risk.

Right now, she is numb.

"I have nothing to give right now," she told me two nights ago.

Drained and depressed, afraid she may lose her life's assets, her world as she perceives it is topsy-turvy. She feels victimized, constantly asking what she has done to deserve what is happening.

Answers to questions like this are difficult.

She is a good woman to the core. Warm and fuzzy, generous to a fault, she takes care of others before herself. Her goodwill is being put to the test.

I know her past. She carries baggage like everyone. Hers is more internalized. She will survive. It is her nature.

307

I'm trained in stress reduction. I can only do so much. All this pain and suffering is real.

Her stress has extended to me.

A vested interest in our relationship, we share an energy bond.

Looking for reasons, those closest to us often lash out.

They need an outlet.

Often, relationships are destroyed in this emotional morass.

Other times, it shifts the other way, and the person feeling victimized turns to their partner for support, encouragement, and love.

Love is the only way through abysmal challenges.

Changing our perception, I see her dilemma as an opportunity. Goodness will prevail as long as we don't get attached to the outcome.

If it all goes to hell in a handbasket, I'm ready and willing to liquidate my assets, move to Mexico, find a villa, and live a simple life together.

She is my muse, a true believer in these words I have written, my technical and moral support.

Hopefully, we will walk through this challenge with the lightness of a stroll on the beach.

Maybe not tomorrow, or next week, but soon the time will come if love leads the way.

I first saw the touring production of "Hair" alone in January 1970,
while job hunting in Coconut Grove, Florida.
Time passes, feelings don't. Been there, and now back again.
Today, 55 years later, I stand with Anne in front of the Lake Worth Playhouse,
after seeing a revival of "Hair."
Pura Vida.

SYNCHRONICITY, PANDEMIC 2020, AND THE STORY OF ANNE

"Time bends, synchronicity weaves,
and even in a world unraveling, love finds its way.
What appears as chance is often destiny in disguise."
— from the Captain's Log

As the saying goes, time flies when you're having fun. This does not include root canals, illness, ptomaine poisoning, STDs, hangovers, hostile relationships, ingrown toenails, and a list that extends beyond jocular contemplation.

Luckily, there is the flip side of this wooden nickel, such as mind-boggling, light-up-the sky sexual and spiritual orgasms, just to mention what comes to mind. (There are many others on this happy-to-be-alive list, but you get the gist without excessive pontification.)

Actually, there is a scientific explanation for why time seems to fly. A recent slight tilting of Earth on its axis could also be a factor. Or, then again, it may simply have to do with our perception and life experiences.

Let's keep this thought process simple and to the point. SYNCHRONICITY.

Things, meaning life, happen that are not explained with a clear causal connection. Kind of like a sleight-of-hand card trick. Or magic! The unexpected occurrence that can permanently alter one's present or future.

In a roundabout way, that's what this chapter is all about. How unexpected instances occur while we are marking time from birth to death that changes the previous status quo. Happens all the "time" (there's that word again).

Say, for example, a safe falls out of the sky missing you by inches and squishes your Pekinese, leaving only a sidewalk stain and tattered leash. Now that's what's called being a lucky mother fucker.

Yes, you're now grieving the loss of a companion that warmed your feet at night while sleeping, but the reality is, another pet store is just down the block.

Now let's cut to the chase. I'm writing these memoirs because I cherish high-adrenaline moments in time over mundane repetition. I dare to be myself, not what others might encourage down the blasé, predictable Path of Mediocrity.

Poet Robert Frost is most quoted from his poem "The Road Not Taken," which ends with the line, "I took the one less traveled by, And that has made all the difference."

Put another way, even the most simple-minded can relate: I opted to take risks and follow dreams and live life to its fullest. With every breath I conspired with molecules and trillions of cells and microbes that comprise this physical body adorned with emotions and feelings and the naïve illusion that we are MORE.

This is why "time" seems to roller-coast in a fairy tale of hits and misses. Why right now, in this very moment, I am a five-year-old wavering down the dirt and grassy driveway, learning to ride a bike, learning one of many lessons ahead. And now, at 82, yet another lesson, writing the life of *Captain Madness*.

Someone who chose uncertainty over white picket fences. Anxiety often above complacency. Always searching for the meaning of life and "Time-less-ness."

The stories you have been reading are authentic. More to come. I took a serious twenty-something-year writing hiatus (for the most part) and need to bring YOU, the reader, up to date as to what has transpired since.

Somewhat an epilogue, but "isn't" because I haven't finished.

In a big way, this chapter pulls together many thoughts and actions, tying "time" to synchronicity and spontaneity.

Living a free life often comes with a price. Being an individual, pursuing your passions and dreams, often is misunderstood as irresponsible (Responsibility actually means "to respond to" any situation).

I had a dream last night about my parents. I was living on my sailboat in Coconut Grove at the time, and it was Mother's Day. And it became the only time they visited during my 15 years of *Living The Life Of Riley* aboard my modest wooden sailboat.

In a moment of gratitude, I reserved them a room at Coconut Grove Hotel across the street from the Marina. It was a toney spot frequented by airline pilots and crew during overnight stays on international flights because of its ideal location, grooviness and proximity to the airport.

Having lived relatively sheltered lives in South Carolina, they were uncomfortable with foreign languages being spoken at the registration desk, so much so that they exited and went down the street to find a less auspicious place. Later, we went back to the hotel for their special poolside Mother's Day luncheon.

Taken aside, I had a rare conversation with my father. He divulged some of the feelings he had been keeping to himself. In his father-son talk he asked, "What am I supposed to tell my friends that my three sons do? One is a drug smuggler on the lam in Australia, my youngest, a tennis pro enticed by the smuggling lifestyle, was caught, convicted, and sentenced to three years in federal prison for smuggling marijuana."

"And me?" I asked, looking him in the eye.

"Why don't you tell them that your eldest son is a part-time college professor in Miami, teaching students about making life choices. And tell your friends he lives on a sail-boat and is a poet," I said. "And tell them that he is happy, un-like many of your friends who you say live in what Henry David Thoreau calls, 'a life of quiet desperation.'"

"Your friend T.J. has a big house lakeside. His game room is mounted with heads of animals that he has proudly killed on Safari for the fun of it. And he's one of the most miserable people that I know."

"So, when someone asks you who you son is, what your sons do, don't forget to tell them about me. I'm happy, healthy, and live an exciting life that the majority of people only dream of. One that generates adventure, happiness, and love helping others."

The moral of the story here is somewhat obvious. It is called KARMA. You always get what you deserve. You always get what you ask for.

And the quaint hotel my parents chose to stay in?

Turned out being a noisy haven for drug dealers.

BUT they all spoke English.

The so-called Pandemic historically started February 2020, changing the world in a way the average person couldn't wrap unravelling brains around. Fear and uncertainty prevailed. People died and cried and went berserk.

Time took on new meaning.

"All we are is dust in the wind."

Those 1970's song lyrics resonated like nothing since the atomic bomb and realization that political forces outside our control frame reality.

Which brings me to The Story of Anne, and how circumstances can turn shit into bitcoins.

My life was on a roll New Year's Day 2020. "The future's so bright, I gotta wear shades," the appropriate song refrains.

A promising, financially secure year (finally!!!) is staring into my pearly blue eyes.

I would be teaching what I like best—living life to its fullest—from Florida to scheduled retreats in Mexico.
I named it *Stress Reduction Immersion and Consciousness Evolution.*

Like a felt-pen stroke, all plans went asunder with COVID-19. You know the history. Everyone does.

Then my beach rental was terminated due to pandemic fallout. As fate would have it, a friend called and referred me to a rental that was in fact less expensive and more spacious, across the street from a huge grassy town park on the Intracoastal Waterway.

Luck of the Irish. Better yet, *Captain Madness* karma.
Call it what it is.
That was June 2020.
The park became my tai chi/qigong court.

If you don't already know, tai chi/qigong is the foundation of all martial arts.

Meditation in motion.

Strengthens the bones and muscles from the inside out.

Qigong is a complete self-guided healthcare system.

Usually I practiced tai chi/qigong early mornings. For once, I decided on August 5 around 7 p.m., to wander down to the water's edge and do another 108-movement tai chi form.

Walking along the path to my destination, I would glance over at the Harbor Towers East condominium, focusing on a condo's wraparound balcony with its grandiose waterfront vista. A location to be relished by any aging seagoing mind.

Then the front door opened, with a woman pushing a cart.

Never one to miss a flirtation, especially considering isolation and lack of usual socializing due to COVID, I yelled up to her: "Champagne and caviar?" She laughed. "Window washing." We bantered for a short while and then continued our destiny. I briefly pondered her essence. Single? Maid? Homeowner? How to meet? Probably unlikely.

Then I noticed, out the corner of my eye, this woman washer looking down, all but consuming my fluid tai chi moves. I pretended not to notice and reflected on an old Buddhist saying that I frequently referred to: "No expectations, no disappointments," and continued my practice.

As I lowered my palms in final tai chi reverence, I turned, and there was Anne. She had raced inside, changed clothes, hastily walked out through security gate and up the path to where I stood, dumbfounded.

"I've been looking for a tai chi/qigong Master for 20 years," she said.

I looked back at her. "You found him!"
We both smiled knowingly.
Like I said earlier: Timing is everything.
We've been together five years now.

In Peace and Love,

Captain Madness

To be continued...